M000078401

EXPAND

A LEADER'S GUIDE TO EXPLOSIVE GROWTH

SAM CHAND

MAURY DAVIS

MARTIJN VAN TILBORGH

JEFF SMITH

Expand: A Leader's Guide to Explosive Growth
copyright ©2020 Dream Releaser Publishing

ISBN: 978-1-950718-58-0

Printed in the United States of America

cover design by Joe Deleon

CONTENTS

INTRODUCTION

Think with us for a moment.

Think of a few key accomplishments in your life. How did that happen? Was it a person who helped you? Was it a place you went? Was it an experience you had? Maybe a book you read?

More than likely, your success was the result of *exposure* to a person, idea, technique, or anything for that matter, which led to an *expansion* of your situation. You met a person and were given an opportunity. You obtained a certificate or degree and a new world opened up. You went to a conference and learned a new way of thinking. Examples are endless. You are thinking of them now.

All expansion is a direct result of exposure.

You expand someone's geography by visiting other places. You expand your historical knowledge by reading and visiting important sites. You grow musical appreciation through exposure to new genres. Cultural diversity is appreciated through exposure to others unlike yourself. Exposure EXPANDS our awareness, thus our capacity!

Leadership is no different. By exposing ourselves to different paradigms, we are challenging our own systems and thought patterns. We don't have to agree on everything but simple exposure to ideas that are not our own, help us to process. Unfortunately, many leaders limit their exposure—thus their expansion—to repetitive voices that they listen to, the books that they read, or conferences that they attend. Leaders tend to circulate in the same circles within their own industries so after a while everyone's got their tribe and their exposure is just looking at the same people. Hence their expansion is limited.

You may be in that position. Or you may know others whose exposure is limited. It may not be something you recognize in yourself but if you pause to consider who or what was the last "outside" voice, thought, or idea you were open to—you might be surprised.

We are here for you! The four of us came together—because we chose to expose our thinking to those outside of our circles—to develop this resource not only as a way to expand your thinking but also as an example of the beauty of doing so. We have unique backgrounds, educations, experiences, and stories to tell. Sam has been serving leaders in a practical way for over 40 years; Jeff has developed the best methods for fostering a healthy, thriving organization; Martijn is able to deliver your message in unique ways utilizing technology; and Maury has engineered a proven process for organizational growth. We came together on purpose because we each recognized that our impact would grow if we listened to those outside of where we were. We were right! Each of us has influenced the others in a unique way and after some years we decided that we needed to share that opportunity. We are here to serve you and to expose you to our worlds, individually and collectively, via Expand.

This book *Expand* is not about a program, it's not about a process, it's not even about a plan. This book was developed to expose you to ways of thinking, questions to ask, processes to embrace, people to develop, growth strategies to adapt and adopt. Exposure.

This book *Expand* will expand your mind only to the degree that you expand your horizons. The purpose of Expand is to push your horizons further because of this fact: everyone stands under the same sky, but not everyone has the same horizons. Some can see further than others and those who can see further from others are expanding because of exposure.

This resource you are reading now is an invitation to expose yourself to new ideas which, we hope, will expand your world! This book is designed for ease of use. We have aimed to make it easy to pinpoint your needs and address them. So, you'll find each chapter and section able to be read and digested independently of each other. Start anywhere and jump around—this is a resource to reference from wherever you are!

PART ONE: PRACTICAL LEADERSHIP

by Sam Chand

1.1

SYSTEMS AND STRUCTURES

IN ANY BUSINESS, church, or nonprofit organization, a clear definition of the need is essential to produce a compelling motivation to succeed. Entrepreneurs notice a gap in the market they can fill by creating a new company or a new product. Pastors are gripped by the reality that a segment of their community hasn't been reached with the gospel of grace. Visionary leaders are moved with compassion to establish nonprofit organizations to meet the needs of distressed people. In each organization, success is defined simply and succinctly. If it's too complex, it can't capture the imaginations of staff teams, employees, and volunteers—and it won't touch the hearts of those they're trying to impact.

THE NEED CREATES THE VISION

Vision isn't born in a vacuum. A leader's vision is the result of being gripped by a palpable need. Who is being bypassed in our community? Who is in trouble and desperately needs help? What products do people want and need? What are the opportunities that aren't being realized, and what are the challenges holding people back?

The need propels the *what* and *why* questions, which shape the leader's vision. After the vision becomes clear, the next question I ask is always: "Who do I need to help me meet this need and make the vision a reality?" It's never *how*, *when*, *where*, or *how much*. I don't think about buildings, budgets, or schedules until I've found the indispensable human resources: a mentor, a coach, or a model I can follow. I ask, "Who has experience I can draw from?" "Who is doing it well right now?" "Who has learned the most important principles I need to apply?" "Who can connect me with the best available resources?"

LOOK AT SYSTEMS AND STRUCTURES

When I talk to people who have been leading for a long time, I notice many of them are frustrated. Business leaders may tell me, "We have good products and a good sales team. Our manufacturing is doing well, and our warehouse gets products out on time. I can't understand why our company isn't growing any faster." Similarly, pastors confide, "We have a talented worship team, people say they like my messages, and we have plenty of good programs. So why are we still stuck at 300 people (or 2000 or wherever their growth has been arrested)?"

They're telling me they're not happy with their size and speed, but they keep doing the same things over and over again, hoping the results will magically change the next time. But it's not exactly the same things—in their frustration, they try to work harder, they ask more from their people, they're a little more intense, and they desperately search for the "missing ingredient" of success. None of these solutions provides more than a fleeting promise of change. In most cases, they're not asking the right questions.

Instead, they need to step back to analyze their systems and structures. If they improve these, size and speed almost inevitably follow. Systems aren't just buildings, programs, products, and budgets. They are *processes* that create and use buildings, programs, products, and budgets to facilitate growth and change. The systems include the organization's platforms, communication tools, and training devices to impart vision, inspire hope to meet the need, and enlist passionate involvement. When the commitment to make systems excel takes root in an organization, every planning meeting, every leadership event, every building, every dollar and every communication becomes saturated with meaning. The organization's systems become well-oiled, powerful machines to accomplish great things.

The structure is the organizational chart of people who work together. We don't just fill in boxes on a chart. We find passionate, skilled people who see the system as an essential tool to meet the compelling need and make the vision a reality.

Systems and structures are inextricably related, and they enable the organization to reach out to touch their community. The beating heart of an organization's systems is the set of connections leaders have with their audience. Do the customers, the people in the congregation, or the needy people in the community believe the organization cares about them? How do we connect with people in the community or our customers? How do we recruit employees and volunteers? How do we develop leaders? Has the senior leader created a culture where employees, staff teams, administrators, and volunteers are enamored with the vision?

Ultimately, all questions are people questions. How do we touch them? How do we draw them in? How do we empower them? How do we make decisions so everyone feels heard and understood? How do we celebrate their accomplishments?

THE LIFE CYCLE OF AN ORGANIZATION

One of the ways to understand the life cycle of any organization is to identify the current position in the order of five distinct phases:

- The *entrepreneurial* (or discovery) phase is the exciting beginning when every dream seems possible.

- The *emerging* (or growth) phase is when the vision begins to take definite shape, leaders are empowered, and the organization sees real progress.

- The *established* (or maintenance) phase is a time when leaders take a deep breath, enjoy their success, and watch their systems function well. But this phase is also dangerous because it can easily lead to complacency.

- The *erosion* (or survival) phase is evident when the organization shows signs of decline, and the earlier vision seems unreachable.

- The *enterprising* (or reinvention) phase is the result of a deeper grasp of the need, a renewed vision, fresh enthusiasm, and new strategies to meet the need. Giving an existing organization a fresh charge of vision and energy is very difficult, but it's essential for future flourishing.

This life cycle of organizations is true in this exact order for businesses, churches, shopping mall, neighborhoods, marriages, and every other type of human enterprise.

At every point in the phases of an organization's existence, leaders need to step back and ask the bigger questions about systems and structures. The fulfillment of their initial hopes for size and speed depends on putting these elements in place, and the turnaround from erosion to enterprising depends on them taking a hard look at their existing systems and structures and making bold new decisions. For instance, instead of assuming you made a bad hire, it might be more productive to assess the process you used: how well you selected, trained, and empowered the person to thrive in the system and structure of the organization. Did you hire to meet a particular need in the system, and did you communicate the specifics of how the person would contribute to meet the fundamental need and fulfill the vision? Did you make the "win" crystal clear to the person? For instance, if you hire an executive for a department of a manufacturing company, what production goals did you set for this person? If you hire a youth pastor, did you make it clear that you expect growth in multiple areas, such as a specific goal in overall attendance by a certain date, the number of volunteers, the level of parent involvement, communication to students and parents, and the number of students who go to summer camp? The goals of increased size and speed are the result of creating and expanding the system and structure in the business, the nonprofit, or the church—and the new hire needs to see the clear connection. Too often, people we hire don't understand how they fit in. We just hire them and hope for the best. This strategy may work for a few bright people who take a lot of initiative, but not for most.

The task of leadership, then, isn't just to give people goals, but to help them utilize effective systems and structures to reach those goals. When we give lofty goals without the underlying framework, we create confusion and pressure . . . and sometimes despair and panic.

The other side of the equation is that some leaders get so fixated on fine-tuning their existing systems and structures that they forget the need and the vision. For instance, the recent trend in education is long-distance learning, which means online classes. Some educators dug in their heels for years because they were wedded to people showing up in their classrooms several times a week. But the goal of providing quality education at a reasonable cost for busy people created a revolution in the delivery system. The need shaped a new, clear vision, which drove innovation in the systems and structures.

Many businesses and churches have fallen in love with "the way we do things around here," so they seldom if ever evaluate them according to the pressing need and the compelling vision. Culture changes, and delivery systems become antiquated in a hurry. We need to stay alert and nimble, always keeping the vision fresh and open to creative new ways of fulfilling it.

CLIMBING OUT OF STAGNATION

If you feel stuck and your solutions are only creating more tension and frustration, I want to offer some words of encouragement:

- You aren't alone! You're in good company! You aren't the first person to feel like your organization is in a rut, and you won't be the last. Others have found a way out of the quagmire of stagnation, and you can too.

- The solution isn't as difficult as you might think. Sure, you've tried a dozen different "sure fire" answers, and none of them brought lasting change. But this time, I'm suggesting a different way of looking at your organization and your role as the leader.

- Identify the need your organization is designed to meet, and clarify the vision to meet it. Yes, you've probably said it a thousand times before, but is it fresh to you? Do you own it? Let it keep you awake at night again with stunning possibilities.

- Then, conduct a thorough analysis of your systems and structures. How are decisions made? How does communication happen? Who has authority and responsibility? Which programs are vital, and which are just nice things to do? Who is passionate about meeting the need and fulfilling the vision? Who has lost zeal and energy? My guess is that you'll uncover the problem through this analysis. The systems that brought you to this point may not be the ones to take you to where you believe God wants you to go. Be ruthless with the analysis. It'll pay off soon.

- Stop doubting yourself, and stop blaming your people. An undercurrent of discontent always surfaces in one way or another, often in passive aggressive behavior. We smile as we point out others' errors—not to help them, but to make sure others know the address of the problem isn't at our door.

- Don't assume you have a powerful and positive culture. Work hard to create the kind of environment where people thrive. An organization's culture—ranging from inspiring to stagnant to toxic—is created moment-by-moment and conversation-by-conversation in messages that communicate meaning and value. Every planning meeting, every board meeting, every performance review, and every interaction of any kind imparts a message about what and who we value. In communication, words carry far less impact than gestures and body language. In the same way, how leaders act communicates more loudly and clearly than the words they say. And the topic and frequency of our celebrations speak volumes about our goals, our hearts, and our willingness to share the spotlight with others.

- Match your stated values with your allocation of time, money, and attention. Our people are watching. If we say our people are our greatest asset but the ones who work closely with us feel ignored or used, we've sent a very loud message that we can't be trusted. But if our hearts genuinely break for people in need and we take time to show love to the men and women we see each day, the people around us will believe what we say about caring for others.

- Look closely at the visible symbols of the organization's culture, such as titles, office allocation, and other perks. How much are leaders held aloof from the rest of the organization, and how much are they approachable and vulnerable? These symbols are declarations of values, culture, integrity, and care.

When we understand that size and speed depend on our systems and structures, we'll pay closer attention to the way things operate and how people are empowered and valued. When we feel stuck, we won't just put our heads down and try harder, hoping for a different outcome. Of course, we'll need tenacity and grit, but we'll add wisdom, insight, and hope to our determination.

Systems must continually adapt to the needs and opportunities of the moment. Static systems gradually lose relevance, but dynamic systems anticipate evolving needs. When I talk to leaders, some of them tell me, "This is how we do things," and I can imagine they've done things that way for a long time. But other leaders explain, "This is how we do things today, but we're always learning how to adapt so we can be more effective as we pursue our biggest goals." Some leaders assume the procedures that worked in the past will continue to work in the future, and they become frustrated when they don't see growth. But other leaders know they need to periodically revisit each of the major systems in their organizations—sales, hiring, marketing, IT, leadership development, volunteer involvement, etc., etc.—so they can stay sharp, relevant, and effective.

STRATEGIC AND TACTICAL

Far too often, leaders and their teams move instantly from a concept to the tactical details, without giving thought to the strategic concerns of the need, systems, and structure.

I believe leaders need to ask and answer five key questions—in this order—when they start any venture, and they need to keep asking them as long as they expect their organizations to grow. Consider the need and the vision for the existence of your organization and ask:

1. Is it sustainable?—Will it last? How long do I want it to last?

2. Is it scalable?—Can it grow? How far?

3. Can it be replicated?—How can it be reproduced? What parts necessarily must be replicated for growth to happen?

4. Is it functional?—How will it be organized? How will we answer the questions of who, how, when, where, and how much? What will be the systems and structures?

5. Is it compelling to others?—How will we communicate the vision and plan? How will we cascade the communication from the top leaders to each tier of influence and involvement?

The first three questions are big picture and strategic; the last two are specific and tactical. People who are starting businesses and planting churches need to begin with the strategic questions and work their way to the tactics. Most leaders of existing organizations spend virtually all their time on the tactical function and communication. They seldom step back to consider the bigger questions. That's perhaps the biggest reason their organizations stop growing (or grow more slowly than they'd like).

Let me summarize: Long seasons of stagnation can be mind numbing. Instead of trying harder with the same systems and structures, I recommend conducting a thorough analysis: clarify the need and the vision so you're captured again by the what and the why, and then spend plenty of time figuring out how you can reconstruct your systems and structures so they can support more size and speed.

1.2

SEVEN KEYS OF CULTURE

Have you ever walked into an office, and after only a few casual, brief conversations with people, you sensed something was wrong? Many of us have a sixth sense about the atmosphere and relationships on a team. Amazingly, some of us who are incredibly perceptive about other cultures are clueless about the nature of relationships and attitudes around us each day. To be objective, we need to step back from time to time and take a good, long look in the mirror. We might be surprised at what we see.

Pastors and business leaders report that it's relatively easy to institute a new program or introduce a new product, but changing the culture is the hardest thing they've ever done. It requires wisdom, courage, and tenacity, but it begins with the realization of the current condition. A few simple metaphors, however, help them see the importance of addressing the culture of their organizations. I often explain that it doesn't make sense to serve a lovely dinner on a dirty plate, and a doctor can't perform a kidney transplant until the patient is free from infection. A stagnant, discouraging, or toxic culture is like the dirty plate and the infection. Very little progress can be made until the plate is washed and the disease is healed. Then, dramatic progress can happen.

A GLIMPSE OF THE CULTURE

I want to invite you and your team to look in the mirror to see the nature of your culture. We'll examine seven important factors that shape organizational culture, and for each of these, we'll identify particular attitudes and behaviors that point a culture toward either inspiration or toxicity. The seven keys of culture are:

Control

Understanding

Leadership

Trust

Unafraid

Responsive

Execution

As we examine these, don't focus on yourself. Instead, take the temperature of your whole team. Culture is about the relationships, communication, and shared values, not just about an individual's perceptions and behavior.

CONTROL

People function most effectively if they are given control (or authority) with responsibility. If they are held accountable for a task without having the means to accomplish it, they'll fail, and they'll be terribly frustrated.

On the other end of the spectrum, if control is concentrated in one person who insists on making virtually all important decisions, the organization experiences a significant bottleneck. Teams thrive when there is a free flow of information and ready access to resources.

Contrary to the beliefs of some people, "control" isn't a dirty word. Delegating responsibility and maintaining accountability are essential for any organization to be effective. Strong, effective teams have a "Goldilocks approach" to control: not too much, not too little, but just the right amount of checks and balances. The right control system for a team is like a conveyor belt of ideas and resources. It manages the flow of work—not to slow it down, but to make it flow smoothly and effectively.

Quite often, the real power broker on a team isn't the person at the head of the table. Good leaders involve everyone in the planning process, but sometimes an angry, sour, or demanding person can dominate a team. A sure sign of problems with control on a team are turf issues. When two or more people believe they have responsibility and authority for a task, they compete with each other for resources, and even more, for supremacy over each other. Turf battles really aren't about the tasks people fight over; they are about personal pride and perceived power.

Team members need to see themselves as partners in a grand venture, not competing for control over others, and not carving out territory to defend to the death, but using delegated authority for the common good.

UNDERSTANDING

Every person on a team needs to have a clear grasp of the vision, his or her role, the gifts and contributions of the team members, and the way the team functions. Each person should be able to clearly articulate each of these vital aspects of the team's life.

Knowing one another and appreciating each person's contributions grease the wheels of progress on a team. How do we know what makes each other tick? By taking time to hear each other's stories. In staff meetings or during an hour over coffee, we can find out more about someone's heart and experiences than we could learn in years of sitting in meetings together. All it takes is a little time and a few caring questions.

Understanding, though, isn't just about the *what* of the organization; it's also about the *why*. Again, grasping the underlying concepts is everybody's job. Leaders need to take time to explain how a new program fits into the plan, why it will make a difference in people's lives, and the important role each person will play in making it successful. Team members are encouraged to take initiative to ask questions so they understand these things, even if the leader forgets to explain them.

LEADERSHIP

Healthy teams are pipelines of leadership development. They recognize that an organization is only as healthy as the pool of rising leaders, so they actively seek to *discover* those who show leadership potential, *develop* resources to equip and inspire leaders, and carefully *deploy* them in roles that enflame their hearts, challenge them to excel, and propel the organization to new heights.

We need to make a distinction between leadership and management. To develop people to become leaders, we focus on heart and character. Training is important, but it's a management issue, equipping people to perform a particular task. Both are significant, but developing people is far more essential in creating a healthy culture than training people in specific skills. Plenty of toxic and discouraging cultures have highly trained, efficient staff members. They know how to do their jobs very well, but their culture stinks.

Team leaders need to be perceptive about how rising leaders are assimilated into the group. Are old leaders threatened, or do they celebrate and mentor the new people? Great organizations enlist existing leaders to be part of the leadership pipeline, offering their insights and expertise, and helping young leaders in every possible way.

TRUST

Mutual trust among team members is the glue that makes everything good possible. Without it, a team quickly disintegrates into a gang of people protecting their turf and forming angry alliances. Trust is important up, down, and across the organizational structure. When people trust each other, they make a strong connection between the vision, their own roles, the input of others, strategic planning, and steps of implementation.

Trust may be freely given, but it is usually earned as people watch each other respond in good times and bad. Integrity and consistency provide a firm foundation for relationships to thrive. Trust is fluid. It takes time to be built, but it can be destroyed in an instant. Trust grows in an environment that is HOT: honest, open, and transparent. People aren't expected to be perfect, but they are expected to own their failures as well as their successes. Confession, contrary to popular opinion, is both good for the soul *and* for the person's reputation.

Failure and times of difficulty are the windows people use to determine if others are genuinely trustworthy. It's easy to put on a happy face when times are good, but struggles reveal a person's true nature. In hard times for an individual, the team, or the organization, the hearts of everyone on the team are exposed. When others fail in an important task, do the leader and team members delight in pouncing on the person who blew it, or do they use the failure as an opportunity for growth? And the person who failed isn't the only one who notices how he's being treated. Everyone on the team is watching, and they are living the experience vicariously, anticipating how they'll be treated when they fail.

Office gossip is one of the most prevalent—and one of the most destructive—behaviors for many teams. Gossip, I believe, isn't innocent fun. It's a form of undercover revenge designed to harm someone.

Trust can be shattered in an instant by a dramatic event, or more often, it is slowly eroded by countless relatively small but abrasive comments and actions. Every team is made up of flawed human beings, so on every team, trust will be an issue to some degree at some time with someone. Depending on the situation, it doesn't have to ruin a team. In fact, relationships that rebuild broken trust often are stronger and healthier than ever before because they've had to be ruthlessly honest, find forgiveness, and communicate better than before.

UNAFRAID

Corporate courage is an incredibly appealing but slippery trait. I marvel at the bravery of soldiers who face withering enemy fire and mind-numbing conditions, but they keep pressing forward until they win the battle. What is the source of their courage? It's not the absence of fear. They face a host of doubts and terrors, but soldiers report that two things keep them going: a clear conviction of the nobility of their cause and a commitment to the men fighting next to them. As I've watched teams over the years, I've seen the same pattern. They aren't fighting a battle against flesh and blood, but men and women on staff teams face difficulties and challenges with courage if, and only if, they are convinced that what they are doing counts for all eternity, and if they believe in the people serving on their team.

Too often, I've met with teams who had a staff member or two who felt they had to walk on eggshells instead of speaking out boldly. For some reason (and it could be any of a host of issues, usually stemming from a painful past, but sometimes more recent wounds in the team environment), they feel insecure, and they believe they need to hide to avoid any risk. Being wrong or being asked a hard question, they assume, is the worst possible fate.

Healthy teams foster the perspective that failure isn't a tragedy, and conflict isn't the end of the world. Great leaders welcome dissenting opinions, as long as they are offered in good will and with an eye toward a solution. These teams are willing to take great risks, and even to fail miserably, because they've gotten over the notion that failure is a personal flaw. When they look at one another, they don't see competitors; they see friends who have their backs as they take big risks. Courage, support, and innovation go hand in hand in inspiring cultures.

RESPONSIVE

Teams with healthy cultures are alert to open doors and ones that are closing. An individual may not notice a particular threat or opportunity, but someone else on the team will. They develop the productive habit of keeping their eyes open so they can handle every situation: on the team, in individual's lives, and in the community.

For teams to be responsive, they have to develop a consistent process for collaboration, with communication lines that are wide open. They value analysis and feedback, and they work on getting and staying aligned with one another. After decisions are made, team members fully support the team's decision. They understand that an individual's foot-dragging or resistance can hold up the entire process, so they learn the art of communication and finding common ground.

Responsive teams don't just focus on big goals and sweeping strategies. They develop the habit of taking care of the little things, such as promptly returning phone calls, responding to emails, and communicating decisions to everyone who needs to know when they need to know it.

Leaders in healthy cultures work hard to disseminate information among the departments and get buy-in up and down the chain of command and between teams. Being responsive requires both a sensitive spirit and a workable system to make sure things don't fall through the cracks. The larger the organization grows, the more energy needs to be invested in being responsive to people inside and out of the team.

EXECUTION

In my conversations with leaders and team members, one of their chief concerns is that teams often talk about decisions but fail to follow through to implement them. When they don't see the fruit of their discussions, they lose faith in each other and become discouraged. It's not a big deal if something doesn't get done because someone was sick or there's another good excuse, but system-wide, consistent failure poisons the atmosphere. Executing decisions is a function of clarity, roles and responsibilities, and the system of accountability.

To be sure that follow-through becomes the norm, leaders need to define goals very clearly. Decisions should be articulated with precision, including who, what, why, when, where, and how.

Clear delegation is essential to execution. The person responsible needs to understand her authority and how to relate to everyone else involved. This person should walk out of the meeting with crystal clear expectations, a plan to coordinate with others, deadlines, and any other requirements.

On some teams, accountability is haphazard at best, but this breeds complacency even among those who would normally be conscientious about following through with their commitments. People don't do what we expect; they do what we inspect. Plans are worthless unless they have target goals, deadlines, access to resources, and a budget. With those things in place, the leader needs to ask for regular updates on the progress.

Developing a culture of accountability takes the mystery and the sting out of giving reports. If everybody is asked to report, then nobody is singled out.

In a culture that executes plans well, the leader is committed to ongoing training to equip team members to achieve the highest goals. Incompetent people are retrained, moved to roles that fit them better, or removed from the team. The organization is committed to people serving in roles that match their strengths. Leaders focus on these strengths, not their weaknesses, and they pursue excellence in every aspect of corporate life, including communication and team building. A relentless pursuit of excellence in execution is a catalyst—not a hindrance—for healthy relationships.

GETTING BUY-IN

One person can change the competition of a team. It's best if the leader grasps the importance of creating an inspiring culture and takes bold steps with the team, but a wise, tenacious team member can begin to create this kind of environment.

Changing a culture requires tremendous patience. We can change boxes on an organizational chart in a moment, but changing culture is heart surgery. It's not only *what* we do; it's *why* and *how* we do it. Culture is about the heart and head, and then it shapes what we do with our hands. Leaders also need a healthy dose of creativity as they take their teams through cultural change. In an article on teamwork, Keith Sawyer, a researcher at Washington University in St. Louis describes the impact of "group genius," the ability of a team to work together to apply creative insights. He says, "Innovation today isn't a sudden break with the past, a brilliant insight that one lone outsider pushes through to save the business. Just the opposite: innovation today is a continuous process of small and constant change, and it's built into the culture of successful businesses."

When people bring their best to the team, amazing things can happen. As the Japanese proverb says, "None of us is as smart as all of us."

1.3

MAKING A GRACEFUL EXIT

Any SUCCESSFUL TRANSITION must involve planning the next steps in our personal journey and assisting whoever succeeds us. It also means confronting whatever anxieties we might have, examining what really motivates us and considering the source of our self-image.

COMMON TRANSITIONAL ISSUES

"The hardest thing," according to one expert in entrepreneurial business, "is figuring out how to let go." It doesn't matter how big or how influential your organization might be, navigating the next step in your transition is going to create some anxiety. It's best to be prepared to confront the inevitable emotions.

When Bill Gates announced his departure from Microsoft for a full-time role running his charitable foundation, his separation anxiety was evident. Gates told Fortune that he got choked up while rehearsing his speech prior to the press conference for his announcement. He worried about leaving the company he founded for something new. "I don't even know what it's going to be like," he said. "I'm taking a risk here that I'm going to miss it very badly."

One of the world's richest men also expressed concern about leaving the security of Microsoft for a new endeavor. "I don't know what it's going to feel like not to come in every day and work 10 hours," he said.

Considering a move away from a high-level leadership role is disconcerting. We may feel as though we're disconnecting from a large piece of our everyday existence and identity. As we depart, we may also feel like we're leaving behind a huge chunk of our status and our self-worth. It's an awkward but unavoidable transition.

Certainly, we can deny or prolong the inevitable day of departure. Media mogul Sumner Redstone, the chairman of Viacom, was 82 years old when he decided to relinquish his CEO role after the company split into two entities. Redstone advised Michael Eisner not to even consider leaving his position as Disney's CEO, despite the board's plans to oust him. "Once you've had this kind of power Michael, let's face it, nobody wants to give it up." Redstone confirmed his attachment to the throne in subsequent comments to Fortune, "My advice in succession is, 'Don't go. Stay!'"

Successfully navigating our personal transitions involves getting in touch with our values and our motivations instead of focusing on externals. It means considering our dreams and identifying precisely who we are. In the end, we can quit a position but we cannot quit who we are. A mover-and-shaker type is going to continue directing traffic and organizing even if they leave a CEO or senior leadership slot to volunteer somewhere.

There are certain things that are part of who you are. Even when you're no longer a pastor, there are talents and gifts that remain part of your nature and your essence. Each of us must find ways to realize what those things are. We must ask ourselves: What would we continue doing even after we relinquish this role or position? Those things are part of who we are. Wherever we are, we will always express those values and those gifts.

Succession planning provides us with an opportunity to face ourselves. We have the privilege of confronting ourselves apart from our everyday work and considering what's important to us. While she describes this inner scrutiny in terms of retirement planning, Betsy Kyte Newman expresses this necessary analysis in her book *Retirement as a Career*.

"The changes that retirement brings can either arrest our spiritual and psychological development or move us to new personal discoveries and a reintegration of ourselves. In retirement, we face ourselves without the burdens and distractions of work; if we stay with the journey, and the fear and pain it brings, we can discover a source of positive power, the path of our true purpose, and the real passion of our lives."

Facing ourselves is a necessary part of successful succession planning. Bill Gates said that his own transition was the result of a decision to "reorganize" his personal priorities, a process that involved "much soul searching." It's about continuing our journey toward a balanced existence. Finding that elusive balance is not about scheduling every minute of every day; it's about discovering and emphasizing what we value. It's about finding our joy and making it our job.

NAVIGATING A NEW TRANSITION

Today's health-care advances have pushed the average life expectancy years to 77 years. That's a significant jump from the 1935 average of 61 years. This increased life expectancy is changing how people think about those years and prompting new thoughts about how to spend that time.

One 60-year old psychologist summed up the meaning of today's different view of the retirement years. "For us, this time is an opening up. In my parents' generation, it was a closing down."

Leaving our current position—by itself—will seem negative unless we are transitioning into some other activity that fully engages our attention. Like Bill Gates—who moved from Microsoft to his foundation—we need some other focus. All of us need to transfer our creativity, our leadership and vision to something else that gives us significance.

It's especially necessary for founders and entrepreneurs to have another focus. If they don't, it's going to be harder for them to keep from interfering. Having too much idle time may cause them to worry that their successors are making mistakes that will destroy what they've built. Working on something else that commands your attention, something that gives you a sense of renewed purpose, fulfillment and meaning will be good for you and for your successor.

Moving forward with a succession plan must involve identifying our motivations and taking some time to tune into our dreams. Once we've spent time planning the organization's future, we must spend time planning our own future. Answering some simple questions can make it easier to develop a clear plan for our lives before stepping down. For example:

- What would I do if weren't running this organization?
- What would I like to accomplish in the next 10 years?
- What would I like to change about my life?
- Do I want to remain close to the work, perhaps in a consulting role?
- How much would I like to travel?
- What volunteer or charity work has always attracted me?

There will be many new opportunities available to us after succession. Developing a plan for our lives as part of our transition planning can help us to take advantage of these new prospects.

SMOOTHING THE WAY FOR A SUCCESSOR

Planning the organization's future and giving ample thought to our own, aren't the only considerations we must make in succession planning. We must also ensure that we gracefully pass the baton to our successor in a positive, affirming manner. It's crucial that we establish the right tone for this change.

What we do and don't do will inevitably send messages throughout the organization. Departing provides us with an opportunity to—as George Barna put it—"set the table" for the leader following us.

One of the best ways to set the stage for a successor is by establishing and adhering to a reasonable but definite departure date. "It's important to know when your work is done," Mark Hurd, CEO of Hewlett-Packard told *Fortune* magazine. "CEOs can stay too long."

It's important to establish and maintain strong boundaries after your departure. Don't allow people to circumvent the new leader. You might even consider letting everyone know that if they send you an email about issues concerning your old position, that you'll be forwarding the message to your successor.

There are situations where it might make sense to remain with the organization, but in another role. This is different from what occurs in large corporations. Unless they also happen to be the board's chairman, once a CEO is replaced, that person typically departs. In smaller organizations and entrepreneurial firms, it's often beneficial for the organization to have the founder around in some well-defined role.

When properly planned and implemented, staying connected to the organization might aid a transition. When handled in a phased approach, this method can be especially reassuring to customers, a congregation and other stakeholders. It's crucial, however, that a departing leader's role be very well defined. Proper planning prevents poor performance. It could prove extremely awkward for a new senior pastor or CEO to establish their leadership while their predecessor is still around, or to have their predecessor reporting to them. How you leave is more important than how you came in.

Whether it's appropriate in your situation to depart or to remain connected, it's always important to honor your successor and do whatever you can to help them rise to the task of establishing the organization's future. Find ways to praise their capabilities to those who remain. Look for opportunities to pass along the heartbeat, the culture and the vision that drive the organization to your successor.

CONSIDERATIONS FOR SUCCESSORS

Succession planning may not be a "slam dunk," but this complex process quickly pales in comparison to the uphill climb facing an incoming successor. After the planning and selection process is concluded, a new incumbent faces the challenges of meeting and exceeding a congregation's expectations, satisfying waiting shareholders or bearing up under the scrutiny of key stakeholders. Filling those proverbial shoes, or making your own tracks, can be daunting.

If you're succeeding an outgoing leader, you may already know that the bookshelves lack specific guidance for your situation. Highlighted here are some ideas and thoughts for your consideration.

ACTIONS TO AVOID: THE DON'T LIST

Don't expect things to be the same for you as they were for your predecessor. If people seem resistant, try not to take it personally. Realize that it's a loyalty issue and that some folks just need more time to adjust to change. You can't expect the same response from people that your predecessor received.

Try thinking of your tenure as a bank account. Any bank account requires deposits. In this case, your stakeholders must make the deposits based on their level of trust in you. Getting that account built up takes time. Your predecessor's years of deposits into the account enabled him or her to get the desired responses. Unfortunately, that account was closed when you became the incumbent; you must now establish your own account. In time, your faithful work will yield similar results.

Don't be quick to make changes for which you lack the necessary relational equity. If you start disassembling everything that preceded you or initiating too many completely new endeavors, it's going to put everyone into a state of shock. People who are in shock aren't going to be too keen on making the necessary deposits into your account.

Sometimes, incoming successors make promises or attempt to cast an organizational vision that's totally unrealistic in an effort to get people behind them. Without a relevant track record with their people, they're going to have a very difficult time.

Incoming leaders must realize that all change is a critique of the past. Even something as seemingly insignificant as painting a wall can be misperceived.

In some cases, new leaders begin taking too many drastic actions. Their people find themselves wondering what was wrong with the way things were and why it was necessary to make so many changes.

It's always better to start small. Since change that's imposed is change that's opposed, focus on building relationships at first. It's vital relationships that will provide you with the equity you'll need for successful future efforts. You can make incremental changes, but be sure to balance those endeavors with getting the necessary relational support. Until you do, you may find yourself writing checks that you cannot cash.

Don't think that people are going to view you like they viewed you before you came. Hard as it may be to believe, there are people who may have wanted a different leadership candidate in your spot. Sure, they were courteous and pleasant when they met with you during the selection process, but they may have had other preferences. Don't rush them; give them time to adjust. Sometimes, they may not have been involved in the entire decision-making process; they may have just received an announcement. You likely have had more time to adjust than they have.

Don't try to be your predecessor. Certainly, you should be respectful toward your predecessor, honoring their accomplishments and their character. If you're following a tremendous leader, one who casts a large shadow, it can cause you to feel compelled to live up to their accomplishments or their reputation. Resist the pressure to become their carbon copy. Your organization doesn't need another person like your predecessor; they need you.

RECOMMENDED ACTIONS: THE DO LIST

Honor and celebrate your predecessor. In many cases, the predecessor who left you an organization to lead is loved and revered. Since people are in the process of shifting their loyalties from that leader to you, it serves you well to honor and celebrate him whenever there is opportunity. As you celebrate your predecessor, you make it easier for people to make their transitions.

Exercise patience. Following a founder, a successful entrepreneur or a much-loved senior pastor is no easy task. It requires self-knowledge and patience, diligence and patience, as well as patience and more patience.

It's important to remember that acceptance can take time. How quickly a successor is accepted varies with the organization. In many cases, acceptance isn't synonymous with arrival. It may help if you can acknowledge the grief and loss associated with the change. Be a realist by acknowledging what people are feeling. Offering them understanding can only help you.

Build relationships with people who have the wisdom to give you advice from the organization's past. Create a counsel of trusted advisors, which is sometimes called a "kitchen cabinet." Realize that you need counsel to help you to make good decisions. Then, connect with the right people. Build good relationships with those that have the experience, the wisdom, and the power and influence.

Take time to understand the shifts within the organization. You may think you know the organization inside and out, perhaps because you were there while you were being developed for your new role. But even though you were in the boardroom before, you were in another chair. Now that you've moved into the first chair, everyone else is relating to you in a different way. When you moved, they changed too.

Because of this power shift, you have to adjust your understanding of the organization.

Be flexible and not overly sensitive. Some people will insist on being your critics. We encourage you to carefully inspect each criticism for some truth that can help you to grow. There is a shred of truth in everything. If you approach criticism from this standpoint, every critic can actually help you to grow into a better pastor, a better leader, or a better CEO.

GROW continually. The letters in the word GROW can provide an easy way to remember many of the important transitions that you'll have to navigate.

- **Grasp** the organizational culture, as every organization is different.

- **Respect** and honor your predecessor, as well as the local traditions and customs.

- **Organize** your strategic thinking and planning while you learn about the organization.

- **Work** at willingness. Be open to criticism, value and seek out the opinions of others.

PART TWO:
HEALTHY ORGANIZATIONS

by Jeff Smith

2.1

ORGANIZATIONAL HEALTH AND LEADERSHIP

ORGANIZATIONAL HEALTH MEANS exactly what it sounds like: the health or wellbeing of an organization. Mckinsey & Co. defines healthy organizations as those that are "high functioning and highly successful over long periods of time."[1] High functioning companies are internally aligned. The departments are all in sync with one another and work symbiotically to support their combined efforts. They execute their objectives decisively and effectively based on research and data. Most importantly, high functioning companies are agile

1. *https://www.mckinsey.com/business-functions/organization/our-insights/organizational-health-a-fast-track-to-performance-improvement#*

and resilient, allowing them to succeed long-term, even as they ride through waves of change.

Keller & Price define organizational health as "the ability of an organization to align, execute, and renew itself faster than the competition to sustain exceptional performance over time."

"Focusing on organizational health is just as important as focusing on the traditional drivers of business performance". Ultimate competitive advantage lies in creating a healthy environment that can adjust to future contexts and challenges, and create a capacity to keep evolving over time.

Patrick Lencioni asserts that organizational health is the single greatest advantage that an organization can have. According to Lencioni, organizational health is about making a company function effectively by building a cohesive leadership team, establishing real clarity among those leaders, communicating that clarity to everyone within the organization and putting in place just enough structure to reinforce that clarity going forward. Lencioni explains that "an organization is healthy when it's whole, consistent and complete, when its management, operations, strategy and culture fit together and make sense. You know you have it when you have minimal politics and confusion, high degrees of morale and productivity, and very low turnover among good employees." Additionally, the value of a healthy organization has a ripple effect that affects all who come into contact with it or its employees.

Henning Streubel, Senior Partner at Boston Consulting Group states in the article, Why Organizational Health is the Key to Competitive Advantage in Business," that his group has analyzed over 1000 companies, across more than 50 countries, to measure the health and "complicatedness" of organizations. Their analysis found seven key indicators of a healthy organization, including: penetration of purpose across the organization, agile organization structure, speedy and effective decision making, cooperation across units to deliver results, high engagement and morale of your people, active development and management of current and future talents, and retention of key talents.

TOXIC ENVIRONMENTS

In the article "Leading Change: Transformation and Organizational Health," Lowy Gunnewiek states that a high functioning team is the essence of organizational health.[2] It emanates as a positive attitude about getting things done, and doing it to the best of one's abilities. It is different than organizational culture. A company's culture is about the way things get done, the shared values and beliefs, and the processes and systems that are used in getting work done.

In dysfunctional companies, a poorly functioning and often toxic work environment finds its way to customers through a disappointing experience with the delivery of a product or service. A disappointing experience encourages existing customers to look elsewhere and deters potential customers from even knocking on the door. Dysfunctional companies are in a death spiral and it is only a matter of time before they "hit the wall"; just remaining a "going concern" becomes questionable.

---

2. *https://medium.com/enernext/leading-change-transformation-and-organizational-health-e7686e7df0be*

Leaders, we must guard our cultures and do whatever we can to restore them and help people flourish. Organizational environments should be purposeful, fulfilling, and life-giving. If your culture has any of the signs listed below, you need to stop everything you are doing and get to work on fixing it with your team (you can't do it alone). If you don't, you run the risk of driving away your people, driving away new people, and driving your organization into the ground.

THE EIGHT SIGNS OF A TOXIC ENVIRONMENT:

PREVAILING NEGATIVITY

The first sign of a toxic culture is a feeling you can sense when you spend time in a workplace where people don't communicate, don't smile, don't joke and don't reinforce one another. You will notice that interactions are more formal than friendly and that no one seems happy to be working there. A visitor or newcomer will feel the dark energy while the employees seem oblivious to it. That makes sense—the fish can't see how murky the water in their fishbowl has become!

STATUS AND TITLE FOCUSED

The second sign of a toxic workplace is that people are very concerned about titles, job descriptions, and levels in the hierarchy. When you meet someone new in the organization, they'll be quick to tell you their title and status. Power (the conferred kind associated with a job title or connections to high-level leaders) is more important to the people working in the toxic environment than the mission they're supposedly pursuing. Status, visibility, and "perks" are more important than success measured by other yardsticks—and more important than the trust level on the team, which isn't even a topic of conversation.

LOW MORALE AND LOW ENGAGEMENT

The third sign of a toxic environment is when morale is low. Typically, this will lead to low engagement. When employees and or members become discouraged, disinterested, or disgruntled it puts stress on relationships and hinders effectiveness and efficiency. Suspicion of others begins to increase and create roadblocks to healthy interaction. Cynicism about the vision and mission prevent total buy in from everyone.

POLICIES OVER PEOPLE

The fourth sign of a toxic environment is that rules and policies are very important. It's more important than the good judgment of your teammates, their combined decades of experience or the rich context of the situation you're dealing with. Everybody is afraid of getting in trouble for breaking the rules, so they keep their heads low and try not to step out of line. Everyone's posture becomes defensive and collaboration is replaced with competition.

SILOS

The fifth sign of a toxic workplace is that of silos. Across the organization there are battles over turf. People become very territorial over personnel, resources, decision making, facilities and more. Internal politics become pervasive.

POOR COMMUNICATION

The sixth sign of a toxic culture is that the informal grapevine is many times more effective as a communications network than any type of official company communication. All too often the organizations information lacks clarity, accuracy, and timeliness. Transparency is also very low.

NO CELEBRATING OF ACCOMPLISHMENTS

The seventh sign of a toxic culture is that employees are overlooked and underappreciated. Opportunities to celebrate contributions to the vision, reaching goals and meeting expectations frequently get missed.

FEAR

The eighth sign of a toxic culture is that fear is palpable in the environment. Doors slam and whispered conversations take place in stairwells. Everybody is concerned with his or her own spot on the company›s constantly-shifting, internal stock index. People are afraid to try anything new or make mistakes for fear of being shamed. They ask one another «Does the big boss like me? What did he say about me?» and fret and worry about who›s up and who›s down. High-level executives jockey for position and shank one another for a favored role or a plum assignment. No one is safe and everyone is on edge.

LEARNING CULTURE

Culture exerts an important influence on organizations and the people who work in them, yet many organizational initiatives address it the least._Culture, in simple term, refers to how things are done in organizations. It is the process of communicating and promoting the organizational ethos to employees, their acknowledgement, demonstration of respect, and cultivates a sense of personal inspiration about one's work. According to Peterson and Wilson (2002), exploring the healthy organization construct should focus on culture because it is a building block for the development of a successful, innovative, productive and above all, healthy organization.

Healthy organizations foster a culture of greater interaction and collaboration where-in employees and managers readily offer their assistance to each other to meet business objectives._Relationship building, therefore, becomes an important element of the culture of healthy organizations. Healthy organizations are characterized by clear and consistent openness to experience, encouragement of responsible risk taking, and willingness to acknowledge failures and learn from them._Healthy organizations are proactive enough to take necessary steps to guard themselves against any environmental contingencies and adapt to technological or operational and market changes._

Leaders and managers across the organization can contribute to a healthier and happier company culture. Claire Zulkey in her article, "Cheers to Your Organizational Health," suggests the following simple checklist to help you gauge areas in which your team or department could use some additional support:[3]

---

3. *https://slackhq.com/organizational-health-definition*

Do the company leaders present a united front?

Leaders should meet regularly to discuss challenges and opportunities, focusing on both the long and the short term. Even when the group does not agree, its members should understand one another's motivations and the benefits of agreeing to disagree.

Is healthy conflict encouraged?

As organizational psychologist Adam Grant points out, when team members feel confident that they can speak their minds without negative repercussions, and when groups can disagree without strife, organizations are more skilled at spotting great ideas.[4]

Is there clarity among leaders throughout the company?

Most workers want to know more about their company and colleagues.[5] Leaders should ensure that they are not only prioritizing their own cohesion but modeling it for everyone. Also, managers should strive to understand the needs and total motivation of their colleagues—the purpose they find in their work and the potential they see for outcomes such as career advancement.

Is transparency an ongoing, consistent conversation?

It's not enough to have an organizational health meeting once a year and assume the work is done. There should be ongoing

4. https://slackhq.com/unlock-your-teams-potential-with-constructive-feedback

5. https://slackhq.com/tomo-today-success-tomorrow-the-key-to-unlocking-total-employee-motivation

conversations among all employees about business strategy, how decisions are made, financial health, promotions, company-sponsored events, industry trends, and overall competitive awareness.

Does your company provide the tools to enable and encourage transparency and connection between teammates?

Weekly meetings to check in, problem-solve, and look ahead take time to plan and execute and are not practical for those who work off-site. Nhi Nguyen of the survey software company Polly talks about how Polly uses a daily recurring survey that asks questions like "What did you accomplish yesterday?", "Are you blocked by anything?", and even a simple, "How are you feeling today?"[6]

COURAGEOUS LEADERSHIP

Leadership that neglects the value of organizational health will, over time, cause companies to become dysfunctional. It is similar to the 3rd law of thermodynamics; systems will revert to their lowest form of energy unless there is an input of energy. Dysfunctional companies are energy destroying!

Committed and courageous leaders are critical to creating a thriving organizational environment. Organizational health starts and ends with the leader. The individual and/or team that set the course for the enterprise. Everyone in the organization should be considered a leader in this process including staff and volunteers along with the senior leader.

6. *https://www.polly.ai/blog/5-workflows-measure-supercharge-team-2018*

Leaders must have "a very deep and persistent commitment to real learning." They must be prepared to be wrong, and ready to acknowledge where they may be part of the problem. They must be willing to bring people together from different parts of the organization and with different points of view. They must champion the creation of a truly shared vision of a thriving workplace and workforce culture. For a leader who is striving for organizational health, focus needs to shift from wanting to control everything to wanting to maximize every relationship.

Courageous leaders are those who have the ability to clearly articulate and demonstrate the organization's vision and bring people along on that journey. Their style is governed by servant leadership as well as the ability to lead with a high level of emotional intelligence, which helps them guide teams through both positive and challenging times. Courageous leaders place a premium on organizational clarity, core values and responsible business practice. In addition, they are committed to the ongoing investment of time, money and manpower in organizational health as a business strategy. The level of leadership has been linked to an array of outcomes such as: morale, safety, climate, and organizational performance. Courageous leaders who are supportive are the catalysts for creating personal and meaningful connections with their employees, which is very critical for bringing about desired excitement and engagement throughout the organization. When the leadership is perceived to be healthy it encourages proper alignment and healthy environments.

In the article, "Company Alignment: The Salesforce Secret to Success," Marc Benioff states that it boils down to these five questions, which create a framework for alignment and leadership:

Vision— What do you want to achieve?

Values — What's important to you?

Methods — How do you get it?

Obstacles — What is preventing you from being successful?

Measures — How do you know you have it?

Vision — What do you want to achieve?

What is the vision for what I want to achieve? That's the first question that must be asked, because if you aren't crystal clear on where you want to go, good luck trying to get "there."[7]

Values - What's important to you?

Ask yourself, "What's important to me about this goal? What are the values supporting the vision?" After making a list of values, I rank them in order of importance. It's an exercise that forces me to choose between pairs of competing priorities — if everything is a priority, nothing is.

Methods - How do you get it?

Establish the methods for implementing your vision and values. This part of the framework outlines all the actions and steps that everyone needs to take to get the job done. You should also rank these methods in order of priority.

---

7. *https://www.salesforce.com/blog/2013/04/how-to-create-alignment-within-your-company.html*

Obstacles - What is preventing you from being successful?

The fourth part identifies the obstacles you might have to overcome to achieve your vision. What challenges, problems, and issues are standing between you and achieving success? Which obstacles are the most critical to resolve, and how will you resolve them?

Measures - How do you know you have it?

Finally, tackle the problem of coming up with the appropriate measures. How will you know when you are successful? In my mind, a subjective yes-or-no judgment doesn't cut it. You need data and metrics to determine what success looks like.

2.2

SAFETY AND TRUST

THE BEST, MOST successful organizations feature highly participatory cultures in which employees routinely identify problems and share and implement ideas. High engagement cultures take a lot of work—the right information, the right team structure, management commitment, training time, and more. But a key factor that is often overlooked is the need to create a safe environment in which people feel comfortable dealing with conflict, taking risks, and trying new ideas.

Psychological safety in the workplace, in simple terms, is the belief that you are safe to take risks around your team—that you can speak your mind without fear. When employees feel psychologically safe, they are empowered to be themselves, and express new and different ideas without fear of reprisal. Without psychological safety, however, fight-or-flight responses often hijack higher brain functions. Perspective and analytical reasoning are siphoned off. Instead, employees perceive pressure by a boss, a competitive coworker, or a dismissive subordinate as more than just workplace challenges; they're experienced as threats. Team members begin to focus on the potential negative consequences of trying new things.

If you do not feel safe in a group, you are likely to keep ideas to yourself and avoid speaking up, even about risks. Furthermore, if mistakes are held against you, you then look to avoid making mistakes thus stop taking risks, rather than making the most out of your talents. Low psychological safety, therefore, gets in the way of both team performance, innovation, learning, and personal success.

Research undertaken by Harvard clearly shows that organizations with a higher level of psychological safety perform better on almost any metric, or KPI, in comparison to organizations that have a low psychological safety score.

In addition to job competency, feedback, resources, productive relationships, and incentives, a supportive work environment is essential to motivate high performance and engagement, and psychological safety is key to this. A positive mental and emotional state elicits trust, inclusion, belonging, curiosity, confidence and inspiration — enabling employees to be more resilient, motivated, persistent, and feel comfortable bringing their whole selves to work.

According to a Pew Research Center survey, 89% of adults say it is essential for today's leaders to create safe and respectful workplaces.[8]

---

8. *https://www.pewresearch.org/fact-tank/2018/09/25/many-americans-say-women-are-better-than-men-at-creating-safe-respectful-workplaces/*

LEADERSHIP AND SAFETY

Leaders have an essential role in creating a safe environment where people can say what they think and not feel attacked. They can ensure that all are heard rather than allowing a few voices to dominate, and they can ensure that new and unusual ideas are not immediately written off but are given a fair hearing. At the same time, people on the team need to learn to express their views in ways that do not threaten the safety of others. This means not just stating an opinion, but researching ideas and bringing facts to the table. People should use the most respectful interpretation of the motives behind what people are saying. Finally, it's essential to end meetings with a path to action.

Laura Delizonna, in her article for the Harvard Business Review, writes about Paul Santagata, Head of Industry at Google and the results of the tech giant's massive two-year study on team performance, which revealed that the highest-performing teams have one thing in common: psychological safety, the belief that you won't be punished when you make a mistake. Studies show that psychological safety allows for moderate risk-taking, speaking your mind, creativity, and sticking your neck out without fear of having it cut off — just the types of behavior that lead to organizational health and achievement. Listed below are the six steps that Santagata took to increase psychological safety at Google.[9]

1. Approach conflict as a collaborator, not an adversary. We humans hate losing even more than we love winning. Santagata knows that true success is a win-win outcome, so

---

9. *https://rework.withgoogle.com/blog/five-keys-to-a-successful-google-team/*

when conflicts come up, he avoids triggering a fight-or-flight reaction by asking, "How could we achieve a mutually desirable outcome?"

2. Speak human to human. Underlying every team's who-did-what confrontation are universal needs such as respect, competence, social status, and autonomy. Recognizing these deeper needs naturally elicits trust and promotes positive language and behaviors. Santagata reminded his team that even in the most contentious negotiations, the other party is just like them and aims to walk away happy. He led them through a reflection called "Just Like Me," which asks you to consider:

- This person has beliefs, perspectives, and opinions, just like me.

- This person has hopes, anxieties, and vulnerabilities, just like me.

- This person has friends, family, and perhaps children who love them, just like me.

- This person wants to feel respected, appreciated, and competent, just like me.

- This person wishes for peace, joy, and happiness, just like me.

3. Anticipate reactions and plan countermoves. "Thinking through in advance how your audience will react to your messaging helps ensure your content will be heard, versus your audience hearing an attack on their identity or ego," explains Santagata.

Skillfully confront difficult conversations head-on by preparing for likely reactions. For example, you may need to gather concrete evidence to counter defensiveness when discussing hot-button issues. Santagata asks himself, "If I position my point in this manner, what are the possible objections, and how would I respond to those counterarguments?" He says, "Looking at the discussion from this third-party perspective exposes weaknesses in my positions and encourages me to rethink my argument."

- Specifically, he asks:

- What are my main points?

- What are three ways my listeners are likely to respond?

- How will I respond to each of those scenarios?

4. Replace blame with curiosity. If team members sense that you're trying to blame them for something, you become their saber-toothed tiger. John Gottman's research at the University of Washington shows that blame and criticism reliably escalate conflict, leading to defensiveness and — eventually — to disengagement.[10] The alternative to blame is curiosity. If you believe you already know what the other person is thinking, then you're not ready to have a conversation. Instead, adopt a learning mindset, knowing you don't have all the facts. Here's how:

State the problematic behavior or outcome as an observation, and use factual, neutral language. For example, "In the

---

10. *https://www.gottman.com/blog/transforming-criticism-into-wishes-a-recipe-for-successful-conflict/*

past two months there's been a noticeable drop in your partic-ipation during meetings and progress appears to be slowing on your project."

Engage them in an exploration. For example, "I imagine there are multiple factors at play. Perhaps we could uncover what they are together?"

Ask for solutions. The people who are responsible for creating a problem often hold the keys to solving it. That's why a positive outcome typically depends on their input and buy-in. Ask direct-ly, "What do you think needs to happen here?" Or, "What would be your ideal scenario?" Another question leading to solutions is: "How could I support you?"

5. Ask for feedback on delivery. Asking for feedback on how you delivered your message disarms your opponent, illumi-nates blind spots in communication skills, and models fallibility, which increases trust in leaders. Santagata closes difficult con-versations with these questions:

- What worked and what didn't work in my delivery?

- How did it feel to hear this message?

- How could I have presented it more effectively?

For example, Santagata asked about his delivery after giving his senior manager tough feedback. His manager replied, "This could have felt like a punch in the stomach, but you present-ed reasonable evidence and that made me want to hear more. You were also eager to discuss the challenges I had, which led to solutions."

6. Measure psychological safety. Santagata periodically asks his team how safe they feel and what could enhance their feeling of safety. In addition, his team routinely takes surveys on psychological safety and other team dynamics. Some teams at Google include questions such as, "How confident are you that you won't receive retaliation or criticism if you admit an error or make a mistake?"

SAFETY AND CONFLICT

One of the most significant things a company must do to create safe organizational environments is to learn to deal with conflict constructively. This enables different perspectives to be voiced, leading to more rigorous thought and better decisions (and avoiding group-think). People get to be heard even if their ideas don't carry the day, so they are more likely to support the prevailing decision. Relationships are reinforced and innovation is encouraged. Anne-Claire Broughton is Principal of Broughton Consulting, LLC offers the following principles regarding constructive conflict.

To encourage healthy conflict, follow a few key principles:

- Emphasize common goals and shared purpose

- Encourage healthy debate via research and facts

- Encourage listening without judgement

- Do not tolerate personal attacks

- Be open to new ideas

- Leaders speak last

SAFETY AND TRUST

Leaders play a pivotal role in building trust within an organization. One of the ways is by being aware of and eliminating what Robert M. Galfold and Anne Seibold Drapeau in their article for the Harvard Business Review call enemies of trust:

INCONSISTENT MESSAGES

One of the fastest-moving destroyers of trust, inconsistent messages can occur anywhere in an organization, from senior managers on down. They can also occur externally, in the way an organization communicates with its customers or other stakeholders. Either way, the repercussions are significant.

The antidotes to inconsistent messaging are straightforward (though they are not easy to implement): Think through your priorities. Before you broadcast them, articulate them to yourself or a trusted adviser to ensure that they're coherent and that you're being honest with people instead of making unrealistic commitments. Make sure your managerial team communicates a consistent message. Reserve big-bang announcements for truly major initiatives.

INCONSISTENT STANDARDS

If employees believe that an individual manager or the company plays favorites, their trust will be eroded. Employees keep score—relentlessly. As an executive, you may think it's worthwhile to let the most talented employee live by different rules in order to keep him. The problem is that your calculation doesn't take into account the cynicism you engender in the rest of the organization.

MISPLACED BENEVOLENCE

Managers know they have to do something about the employee who regularly steals, cheats, or humiliates coworkers. But most problematic behavior is subtler than that, and most managers have a hard time addressing it. Consider incompetence. Anyone who has spent time in business has encountered at least one person who is, simply and sadly, so out of his league that everyone is stupefied that he's in the position at all. His colleagues wonder why his supervisors don't do something. His direct reports learn to work around him, but it's a daily struggle. Because the person in question isn't harming anyone or anything on purpose, his supervisor is reluctant to punish him. But incompetence destroys value, and it destroys all three kinds of trust.

Then there are the people with a cloud of negativity around them. These are often people who have been passed over for promotion or who feel they've been shortchanged on bonuses or salaries. They don't do anything outright to sabotage the organization, but they see the downside of everything. Their behavior often escapes management's attention, but their coworkers notice. After a while, people tire of their negative colleagues and may even catch the negativity bug themselves.

And, finally, people who are volatile—or just plain mean—often get away with appalling behavior because of their technical competence. Extremely ambitious people, similarly, tend to steamroll their colleagues, destroy teamwork, and put their own agendas ahead of the organization's interests. In both cases, ask yourself, "Is this person so valuable to the company that we should tolerate his behavior?"

Sometimes problematic employees can be transferred to more suitable jobs; sometimes they can be coached, trained, or surrounded by people who will help them improve; and sometimes they must be let go. The point is that they can't be ignored. Every time you let troubling behavior slide, everyone else feels the effects—and blames you.

FALSE FEEDBACK

Being honest about employees' shortcomings is difficult, particularly when you have to talk to them about their performance regularly and face-to-face. But you must do it. If you don't honor your company's systems, you won't be able to terminate employees whose work is unacceptable. What's more, employees who are worthy of honest praise will become demoralized. "Why should I work this hard?" they will ask themselves. "So-and-so doesn't and everyone knows it, but I happen to know we got the same bonus." You won't hear the complaint directly, but you'll see it in the lower quality of the competent employees' work.

FAILURE TO TRUST OTHERS

Trusting others can be difficult, especially for a perfectionist or a workaholic. When managers don't give them that chance, the organization loses the trust of those employees, and the more talented among them leave.

ELEPHANTS IN THE PARLOR

Don't ignore things that you know everyone is whispering about behind closed doors. Bring such issues out into the open, explain them briefly, and answer questions as best you can.

Don't be afraid to say, "I'm sorry, I can't offer more detail because that would violate a confidence." People will, sometimes grudgingly, accept the fact that they're not privy to all the gory details. But their trust in you will decline if they suspect you're trying to conceal something.

RUMORS IN A VACUUM

Temporary information vacuums in corporate life are common, and distrust thrives in a vacuum. What can you do? Be as up-front as possible—even if that means telling employees you can't say for certain what's going to happen. And be aware that the less you say, the more likely you are to be misinterpreted.

You don't have to be a chatterbox to counter this enemy of trust, but do try to put yourself in your listeners' shoes. What don't they know about the situation at hand, and how will that affect what they hear? Are you saying enough? Or are you speaking in shorthand, either because you feel you can't share more information or because you assume people will understand what you're getting at?

CONSISTENT CORPORATE UNDERPERFORMANCE

If a company regularly fails to meet the expectations set by its senior management team, trust erodes rapidly. Look at Kodak, Polaroid, and Xerox in times of decline. When an organization's performance is weaker than expected, a growing number of employees at all levels fear for themselves on a daily basis. They spend less and less time thinking for the organization and more and more time planning their own next moves. What can you do? Be realistic when setting expectations and communicate as much as possible to all employees about why you're setting these goals and how the company can meet them. The more knowledge people have about what lies behind expectations, the more likely they are to continue trusting you and the company, even in tough times.

Organizational Health demands safety and trust. Without these key elements, organizations devolve into fear and cynicism that stifles collaboration, creativity and effective communication. Successful leaders are not only cognizant of the importance of safety and trust but they consistently and actively take steps to cultivate these elements to create healthy environments.

2.3

CLARITY AND COLLABORATION

ORGANIZATIONAL HEALTH IS much more than profit and loss. As McKinsey & Company summarizes it, the health of an organization is based on the ability to:

- Align around a clear vision, strategy, and culture

- Execute with excellence and efficiency

- Renew the organization's focus over time by responding to market trends and remaining relevant through innovation

According to Peter Lencioni, organizational health is about making a company function effectively by building a cohesive leadership team, establishing real clarity among those leaders, communicating that clarity to everyone within the organization and putting in place just enough structure to reinforce that clarity going forward. To accomplish this requires implementing the following disciplines:

DISCIPLINE 1: CREATE CLARITY

In addition to being behaviorally cohesive, the leadership team of a healthy organization must be intellectually aligned and committed to the same answers to six simple but critical questions and there can be no daylight between leaders around these fundamental issues:

- Why do we exist?

- How do we behave?

- What do we do?

- How will we succeed?

- What is most important, right now?

- Who must do what?

DISCIPLINE 2: OVER-COMMUNICATE CLARITY

Once a leadership team has established behavioral cohesion and created clarity around the answers to those questions, it must then communicate those answers to employees clearly, repeatedly, enthusiastically and repeatedly (that's not a typo). When it comes to reinforcing clarity, there is no such thing as too much communication.

As tempting as it may be, leaders must not abdicate or delegate responsibility for community and reinforcement of clarity. Instead, they have to play the tireless role of ensuring that employees throughout the organization are continually and repeatedly reminded about what is important.

DISCIPLINE 3: REINFORCE CLARITY

Finally, in order for an organization to remain healthy over time, its leaders must establish a few critical, non-bureaucratic systems to reinforce clarity in every process—hiring, managing performance, rewards and recognition, employee dismissal—that involves people.

These disciplines may sound idealistic—and they are—but health is a matter of degrees. Any improvement will reap benefits. There will always be those that use "idealism" as an excuse to not make the effort; to find this all too remarkable to actually implement. Not surprisingly, the key is leadership. But it is a sacrifice.

From an article in McKinsey Quarterly Lili Duan, Rajesh Krishnan, and Brooke Weddle write that the following enhances clarity in an organization:

Set a Clear Direction

Health in a transformation starts with strategic clarity and a shared vision that has been translated into crisp goals and milestones. The translation process helps the company decide what it will and will not do (including where it will and will not compete). And the broad communication of it to leaders and employees helps them avoid working on initiatives that are not germane to the strategy or that might even send mixed signals about what the strategy is.

Make It Meaningful to Employees

The companies that made the biggest gains on health in a transformation took the extra, critical step of ensuring that their employees' day-to-day behavior was guided by the company's vision and strategy. This requires thinking through how to match the personal goals of employees with the company's goals—going beyond "cascading" the strategy into key performance indicators and targets to involving employees up front in setting the company's strategic objectives, ensuring that the right talent is in place to achieve those objectives, and making sure that each individual's "stake" in the strategy reflects his or her aspirations.

Build strong operational discipline, in a supportive way organizations seldom get fit without strong operational discipline. It's important to start at the top, with explicit targets for operating performance that are then replicated at other levels. Operational discipline requires the communication of clear standards of work so that employees understand how to achieve goals and metrics consistently. This also helps leaders ensure that the day-to-day work complies with those standards, and it allows leaders to emphasize the core values of efficiency and productivity. Maintaining operational discipline puts a premium on another management practice: supportive leadership, which includes creating a sense of teamwork and mutual support throughout the organization and demonstrating concern for the welfare of employees.

The first (and often most significant) impact a transformational leader can make occurs by defining and clarifying an organization's values. This may come in the form of cleaning or updating its mission and vision statements or simply ensuring there is a clear difference between the two. Transformational leaders can step into a new organization, identify what isn't working, and come up with a strategy and set of recommendations to solve it.

In order to begin to formulate these skills, aspiring transformational leaders should simply begin to familiarize themselves with this type of process. Identify the vision and mission of your current organization and begin to draw conclusions to determine if, from your position, those values are being supported by every division within the company. If they are being supported, try to identify what strategies executives are utilizing to accomplish this. You may also consider these leaders as potential coaches and mentors and work to mirror their leadership styles. If they aren't, consider ways you might approach rallying the organization together to reach those common goals. While it is important to be wary of your company's leadership infrastructure and how they may react to such suggestions, Stein encourages aspiring leaders to remember that, "transformational leaders don't wait for change to happen—they create it."

COLLABORATION FEEDS ORGANIZATION HEALTH

Collaboration can energize organizations by increasing employee engagement, improving retention, and increasing innovation. It can help employees thrive in a constantly changing, diverse workplace. As organizations expand, however, employees are moved through telework and multiple locations, budgets shrink, and workloads expand, making collaboration difficult to achieve. Unfortunately, many senior leaders see collaboration as a skill that is only applied to certain projects rather than as a cultural value that is established throughout the entire organization and that should be embedded in the company's fabric.

What Is Collaboration and How Does It Benefit the Bottom Line?

Collaboration is usually viewed as an activity that involves team members working on a project together. True collaboration is more than an activity, however. It is a process with behaviors that can be taught and developed. It is a process governed by a set of norms and behaviors that maximize individual contribution while leveraging the collective intelligence of everyone involved. It is the way in which people collectively explore ideas to generate solutions that extend beyond the limited vision of a single person.

Organizations have conventionally applied collaboration to teams or organizational levels (such as senior leadership) to break down silos, to foster cross-functional activities, and to encourage better innovation. This type of collaboration can yield positive results. In addition to increasing innovation, collaboration increases employee energy, creativity, and productivity, which generally leads to less stressed, happier, and more engaged workers.

As many organizations can attest, however, when collaboration is focused only on teams or a single organizational level, it is extremely difficult to sustain, and this makes the benefits of collaboration fleeting. True organization-wide collaboration can provide sustained benefits such as:

Fully engaged workers who are eager to take on new projects and challenges and who embrace change.

- Improved organizational flexibility and agility.

- Improved employee health, wellness, and performance.

- Extremely high retention rates.

- A competitive advantage when attracting top talent.

- The ability to develop and bring products faster to the market.

- Increased top-line and bottom-line.

Organization-wide collaboration can spark new life in a company and motivate employees. Sharing new ideas and knowledge lets others see things from various perspectives, encourages them to work in new directions, and advances the organization forward.

Collaboration is an important indicator of organizational health. Organizations that work well together perform better and they are more fun to be a part of. To achieve this advantage, according to an article from Integris Performance Advisors, teams must dedicate effort towards mastering the following five specific behaviors.

1. Focusing on Achieving Collective Results

Why do we need teams in the first place? Because teams can accomplish things that individuals on their own can't. So, the ultimate measure of success for any team is the results it produces.

It is important to keep focus on results and meeting the pre-determined goal.

2. Holding One Another Accountable

In most cases, a team will reach its goals only when everyone does his or her job. Therefore, our ability to achieve collective results is reliant not only on our own efforts but also on the efforts of others. Then it should naturally follow that it is the responsibility of every member of the team to push every other member of the team to do his or her best. So even though we know we are relying on each other we must overcome the uncomfortable and sometimes awkward moments that come with holding one another accountable.

3. Committing to Decisions

There is one simple concept that makes all the difference in the world when it comes to holding another person accountable for something…did the parties commit to the decision in the first place? If we have not established clarity around our shared expectations and gained agreement on our respective roles and responsibilities, then the idea that we would be willing to hold each other accountable is absurd. Teams must emphasize committing to decisions about direction and priorities as a precursor to expecting people to put pressure on their peers to perform.

4. Engaging in Conflict Around Ideas

There is a saying that people must "weigh in to buy in." If we are going to ask all members of a team to truly commit to a shared vision, then we need to be certain that we get all the ideas (and emotions) out on the table. And the only way to make sure that all voices are heard is by having the team be collectively willing to engage in healthy and respectful conflict around ideas. Although many teams struggle in this area, we logically know it's a good idea to discuss different ideas and points of views.

5. Building Trust With One Another

Putting your own ideas out there, especially when they go against the direction of "bolder" personalities or the group as a whole, can be a difficult thing. When team members are fearful of attacks or are uncertain about how others will respond, there's a natural tendency to hold back and just stay quiet; to protect oneself and not show vulnerability. But there is one key element that enables teams to push past the typical discomfort of associated with conflict: it's called "trust." According to Webster's dictionary, one definition of trust is the belief that someone is good or honest. Applying this definition to our purposes here, we can say that trust is the belief that my team mates are good, honest and ultimately have the best of intentions. When teams dedicate focused effort on learning to be vulnerable with each other, the result is a domino effect that enables the team to....

- Build Trust with One Another, which enables the team to…

- Engage in Conflict Around Ideas, which enables the team to…

- Commit to Decisions, which enables the team to…

- Hold One Another Accountable, which enables the team to…

- Focus on Collective Results, which enables the team to…

LEADERSHIP AND COLLABORATION

The role of the leader plays a pivotal part in establishing the framework for collaboration within an organization. The impact of not only the systems that they implement but also their example will shape the environment of the organization in this area in a significant way. According to Brett Cooper, President of Integris Performance Advisors, leaders should seek to take the following actions:

When leaders align their actions with shared values and set a personal example of what they expect from others and model the desired behavior, others on the team are more likely to follow suit and also start to become more open and trusting.

When leaders put a priority on inspiring a shared vision based on common aspirations, it pushes everyone on the team to commit to the decisions the group has made.

When leaders make it a priority to challenge the process and search for innovative ways to change, grow and improve, the team is motivated to share their opinions and engage in robust dialog around a full range of ideas.

When leaders enable others to act by promoting cooperative goals and sharing power and discretion, individual team members recognize that it's up to everyone to support each other and hold each other accountable for what's been agreed upon.

When leaders encourage the heart by showing appreciation and celebrating team victories, it serves to focus all team members on achieving collective results.

One of the greatest takeaways regarding collaboration is that it can make life so much more enjoyable. Yes, collaboration can make employees and volunteers more productive and benefit customers. In addition, collaboration also gives employees and volunteers the opportunity to feel more connected to their jobs and co-workers, reduces stress at the workplace, makes their jobs easier, allows for more flexibility, and in general makes them happier as people. This means less stress at home, less arguments with spouses, and more time to enjoy and be present with loved ones. Collaboration not only positively impacts the lives of employees while on the job but also after they leave the office.

PART THREE: STRATEGIC GROWTH

by Maury Davis

DESIGNING GROWTH

GROWTH

THE FIRST WORDS ever heard by the human ear were, "Be fruitful and multiply." When I had my God moment in 1975, the directive to grow motivated me and drove me to levels of passion I never knew existed. Yet, I discovered that passion without the proper tools causes you not only to burn the candle at both ends, but also burn out. Strategic thinking, paradigm shifts, cultural relevance, and generational challenges never figured into my start as a pastor. Sometimes the excitement of the moment can rob you of anticipating the challenges of the journey.

I took a small church to mega church status, but it came with the price of unnecessary stress, conflict, and inner turmoil. Once I reached the pinnacle of my dreams-come-true, I discovered the plateau—that moment when, after twenty years of incredible growth, victories, and achievements, nothing I did worked. I revisited old ideas. I renewed passion for things that historically made a significant difference, and nothing I did moved the needle. I was stuck, unable to move forward and refusing to move backward, spinning my wheels in circumstances I couldn't control.

You see, you can have dreams of fruitfulness, yet fail to multiply. You can multiply and grow quickly, but with no fruit or substance or truth, it is meaningless. You must have fruitfulness to make a difference, and you have to grow to keep from being a "flash in the pan" or a momentary trend. I had dreams, but I couldn't multiply. I couldn't figure out how to increase the platform of my message. I didn't see the correct resources or structure that would transcend cultural relevance and all of those other challenges we never faced before.

I suppose leadership at one time meant muscles; but today it means getting along with people. —Indira Ghandi

Flabbergasted, frustrated, and in all honesty, anxious, I realized I needed something or someone to come alongside me and help me discover the way out of being stuck. I knew status quo was not acceptable to God and certainly not to the people who had trusted me to lead them from victory to victory, not from same-old to same-old. I have a conviction that God orders our steps and guides our paths. He doesn't order our resting spot. He doesn't guide the couch while we sit on it and do nothing. God is a God of action, of forward movement. In order for the Lord to direct our steps, we have to be moving ever forward, seeking His will. I hired a coach and a consultant to work with me. My future was radically changed. Three things happened:

- I learned to think and process leadership in a totally different way.

- I learned to develop the staff rather than micro-manage them.

- I learned to empower lay-leaders to perform at a different level.

These three chapters will cover the THREE PILLARS of future fruitfulness that are necessary for growth, health, and reward.

I hope these pillars encourage you and challenge you to remain diligent in your pursuit to bear fruit and grow, that at the end of this journey called life, we would all be able to repeat the words of Paul in Galatians 1:24 (NASB). "And they glorified God because of me."

THE PRIMARY LEADER

From the time I found my start in ministry, the majority of people in my circle of friends and colleagues dreamed of being the Lead Pastor. Many people dream about leading and running their own business or arising through the ranks at an established company to be president. They dream of what they would do, how they would lead, and the changes they would make. My point is that most people have a passion to make a difference, to achieve a different level of success, to be recognized for their talents, brilliance, and creative ideas. Very few of us who have had that dream and accomplished it realized the weight of the lead position, the responsibilities that came with it, and the challenges or the pain involved.

There is a significant difference in any chair that isn't the main chair. Back-seat drivers always do it better. Monday morning quarterbacks always win the game. Second guessers always believe they should have made the decision, but the achievements are always illusions. I can say that because I have done all three. After sitting in the lead chair, I discovered the very same ideas I knew would work, didn't. The results I imagined actually evaporated right before my eyes.

Every leader has asked themself the question, "How can I overcome being stuck, frustrated, plateaued, and denied the success of my goals?" Much like the children of Israel in the wilderness, we get tired of going around the proverbial mountain. True visionary leaders cannot tolerate a lack of progress. So, how do we move forward when we don't have the answers?

Moving forward will always require change, and moving forward successfully will always require introspection. Retrospection is easy. There's no risk, and you don't have to do it alone. All those other chairs are more than willing to offer the primary leader recaps and opinions and ideas. Introspection can only be done by you. But let's break the myth that it has to be done alone. I hired Dr. Sam Chand to come alongside me and help me find a way out. What I didn't know about hiring an executive coach whose whole passion is to be a "Dream Releaser," is how much work I would have to do on myself. He didn't focus on the organizational structure. He didn't focus on staff evaluations and reassignments or even on staff development. He focused on me.

It was only through changing myself, my thought process, my demeanor, and my decisions that I was able to pull myself off the plateau and see forward momentum again.

As a pastor who has transitioned to become a life coach and church consultant, I have learned to focus first and foremost on the Lead Pastor's personal development and transformation.

The snare of stagnancy is that between our formation and aspiration, mental institutionalization sets in. We get trapped in the mindset that what used to work will always work and what worked in the past will work forever. Success doesn't come from stationary people.

When we look in the Bible at the story of Ruth and Orpah—both daughters-in-law to Naomi—we see that when the time came, Naomi told Ruth and Orpah to leave. The women had vastly different reactions. Ruth kissed her mother-in-law and said, "Where you go, there I will go…your God will be my God." Orpah kissed Naomi goodbye and returned to Midian, the land of her people. Orpah didn't change. She chose to remain stagnant in the past. Midian is a place where nothing ever changes. Ruth, who embraced change, gave birth to a King—David. Orpah, who rejected change, gave birth to a nightmare—Goliath. Stagnancy will always bring an obstacle into your future. Repeating decisions and actions because they used to work is a natural human reaction to a problem. However, dreams don't come from that which does not change. Traditional, historical, denominational thinking is the most common barrier to the future you dream of.

"What got you where you are will not take you where you want to go." —Ron McManus

Every one of us must battle institutional thinking, and God has no problem doing His part in that battle. He can miraculously set you free, promote you, and place you in the position and land of opportunities beyond your dreams rather than a place of oppression where your heart's desires are stifled and seem to be dying. He can deal with the "Egyptians" in your life and the experience of suppression, persecution, and bondage. You can't disqualify yourself from God's calling. He's bigger than that. But you can affect the effectiveness and efficiency of your journey.

In 1 Samuel, one of the first examples of institutional thinking, the Israelites wanted a king. I can only imagine that this grieved God, that they shouted for an intermediary on Earth rather than abide under the King of Kings. After a warning, God told Samuel to appoint the king. It created an enslavement to authority and government.

I thank God for organizational structures and unity through like-minded believers. However, I think it's important to mention, that we as leaders are not here to be the king. We're here to be the shepherd. We're here to manage the people and resources to bring glory to God. And as long as we remain submitted to God and steadfast in prayer and seeking His will, we are only indebted to God. Oh, what a Master He is. Institutions and denominations and history all have a place, but the true voice in moving forward is God's. What is He calling you to do and who is He calling you to do it with?

A leader…is like a shepherd. He stays behind the flock letting the most nimble go out ahead, where upon the others follow, not realizing that all along they are being directed from be-hind. —Nelson Mandela

Introspection is scary. It's almost like not knowing what we will encounter. We have to look at our failures and weaknesses even more than our successes and strengths. It's painful and difficult. Changing ourselves is truly the only way to effect change around us when we are stuck.

What a shame that when I was on the plateau, the last thing I thought to change was myself. Constantly learning, growing, and introspecting, constantly evaluating ourselves for improvements … that's the only way we can avoid becoming stuck in the first place. Without introspection, the primary leader is relying on crisis-management. Everything is a reaction. When the Primary Leader is growing, the dream can grow, too. When the leader is right, you're not having to manage a message. You are the message.

History is a beautiful thing. It gives us access to some of the greatest minds of the world. When I look at the most successful people in their industry, I see a commonality. They all show incredible daily discipline in improving themselves, whether it's intellectually, emotionally, spiritually, or physically. Maya Angelou needed such a separation of home and work that she rented a hotel room daily and wrote from 7 a.m. to 2 p.m. with nothing other than a Bible, playing cards, and a drink. In a world that praises multi-tasking, her mastery of single-tasking won Pulitzers, Grammys, a Tony, and left a mark on the literary world. Ben Franklin had an appointment every night to record his daily good and frustrations. His journals are filled with analysis. Bill

Gates will take around 20 books on a short retreat, ever educating himself. There is not a long-standing successful person out there in any capacity who is not investing in their own personal growth.

Step one for a primary leader to overcome institutional thinking is to be confident enough in their resources, their team, their leadership, and the voices they allow to have input, to break the mold. The only way to gain that confidence is to be in control of their own personal growth through constant introspection and self-correction.

A good leader inspires people to have confidence in the leader. A great leader inspires people to have confidence in themselves. —Eleanor Roosevelt

The Primary Leader controls the life and death of the operation.

When I think about incredible leadership, I think about leaders like Luis Urzua. In 2010, the world watched in terror as 33 miners became trapped underground for 70 days. Luis Urzua was the shift manager that day, and he very quickly became the owner of the mine. He organized the men and supplies into a refuge cavern and quickly began formulating maps and information to aid in the rescue. Then he addressed his men's emotional needs.

The Chilean Minister of health has described mining leadership as a military operation. He emphasized a rigid system of power with military hierarchy. Luis had to deviate from that institution. Luis has said he relied on speaking the truth and democracy. He very quickly set up a majority vote process for decisions. He assigned jobs and encouraged the men daily. Luis Urzua is an exceptional leader who was in tune with his own resources and mentality enough that he was able to remove himself from institutional thinking. He saved lives when applying historical techniques would have literally left him stuck forever underneath the desert.

I love stories of people who rebel against stale institutional thinking to change the tide. Princess Diana began a conversation on compassion when she opened an AIDS/HIV clinic in 1987. There was still a lot fear and stigma and confusion in the 80s. She shook a patient's hand without a glove on. That one small act— not even a word was spoken—impacted the trajectory of human kindness. Rosa Parks sat down. She changed the trajectory of discrimination that day. She changed the trajectory of a race. Warren Buffet has a notoriously hands-off management style that gives employees ownership and directly contrasts with his competitors' management culture. The people in Jerusalem waited for decades in turmoil before Nehemiah told them to build a wall. It was built in 52 days. All of these people who dared to do things differently from their institution should be a lesson to us in making an eternal impact. It all starts with someone who will lead a conversation, lead a movement, lead a company or church. It all starts with a leader.

The primary leader is the catalyst for becoming unstuck. If they are not growing, the dream is not growing. If they're stuck, eventually the dream will be trapped right along with them. The key is remembering that our people don't work for us. We work for them. And we can't develop others unless we are developing ourselves.

THE QUESTION

Are you ready to change enough to accept new responsibilities and priorities that produce promotion, prosperity, and freedom from frustration?

3.2

DESIGNING EMPLOYEES

To win in the marketplace, you must win in the workplace.
– Doug Conant, CEO Campbell's Soup

HAVE YOU EVER had a misconception? Yes! Have you had an untested belief that you were absolutely sure would work and then it didn't? I have! Has your thinking ever been deceptive? Mine has!

When I began the journey of building the church and the organizational structure that would take it to the highest levels of fruitfulness and productivity, I had a number of false beliefs that time and people proved wrong over and over again. I discovered that hiring employees is like having children. When my wife and I found out she was pregnant with our first child, I developed a serious sense of expectation for the child. We were four months into the pregnancy when we were told that my wife was not having a single baby, nor was she going to give birth to twins, but that she would be the proud mother of TRIPLETS. After the shock and the process of emotional out-pouring to God and family, I re-thought raising three at once. I never forgot what my dad said the night we broke the news to the family. He said, "You need to be glad that you don't already have a child." I asked, "Why?" He said, "Because you have no idea how hard this is going to be." He was absolutely right. I never dreamed of multiple nighttime feedings that never seemed to end and arising in the morning to do my part ... make 24 small bottles for my wife for the daytime feedings of preemies. Bath time was never as easy because one always wanted to cry or tinkle in the water. Changing diapers for the girls was okay, but, with a boy, you never knew when you were going to be assaulted with unexpected body fluid. I loved those babies, but expectations and reality were two totally different scenarios. As you learn, live and hopefully love, you learn to identify the wrong thought processes and replace them with more productive ways of thinking. In the beginning of any new endeavor, you truly are operating on theories and not experience.

Let me give you some of my assumptions from the beginning of building my team:

- Every person I hired would bond with our congregational members.

- Every person I hired would be a team player.

- Every person I hired would be a high-level performer.

- Every person I hired would be incredibly cognitive in their leadership and decision-making.

- Every person I hired would be teachable and humble.

- Every person I hired would have the same level of passion for the organization I had.

- Every person I hired would pursue and produce excellence in every area.

- Every person I hired would be grateful for a job.

- Every person I hired would leave their personal problems at home.

- Every person I hired would fulfill their contractual agreement.

- Every person I hired would anticipate the needs of our congregants/customers.

- Every person I hired would be emotionally stable, financially healthy and relationally professional.

- Every person I hired would enthusiastically embrace my vision and leadership.

I knew from the beginning that there was a limit to what I could do by myself. But I learned quickly—the greater truth—that I was limited by the people I hired, the way I hired, and how I trained them. If you hire the wrong people, fail to manage the right people, or fail to develop your team, your opportunity to grow and succeed is severely reduced. You may be able to get the job done, but it will be at the expense of your health and mind and without fulfilling much of the potential.

Retrospection is important, but the question at hand is not, "What did I get wrong?" The real question is: what can we do to avoid unrealistic expectations in the future? Realizing there are no perfect people, what are realistic expectations? How do we choose our employees more accurately? How do we train them more effectively? And HOW do we empower them more efficiently?

Below are three steps to building a great team. These steps came from much reflection, consultation with successful leaders around me, and feedback from employees on what I could have done better.

THREE STEPS TO BUILDING A GREAT TEAM

THE HIRING PROCESS

Let me give you a word that I haven't always practiced, but I learned both the hard way and through personal coaching with Dr. Sam Chand. **PROCESS** is both a plan and a producer of greater things. As I have studied and researched, I have discovered that there are much better models of hiring than I used and that many people use.

Background checks are critical. Not just criminal of course, but a full exploration into a candidate's background with prior employers. Take the time to write down the most important questions. Listen to their answers, but more importantly, listen closely to what is NOT being said or even deflected. Many times, a person is afraid of lawsuits, repercussions or being dragged into drama, so they avoid the blunt truth. Take the time to look at the employment history and longevity by which a person has held previous jobs. You would not expect a high school graduate or a college student to have a long tenure, but a person who is middle-aged should have a track record of stability and a record that is measurable and demonstrates increased responsibility and growth in duties.

Assessing someone's skills is not difficult. Determining their work style, personality, potential, and relational aptitude is more difficult, but exponentially more important. Skills can be taught and trained into someone. Integrity, clarity, energy, and IQ can't be taught. I am reminded of my daughter's favorite childhood book, *A Wrinkle in Time*. The children are accompanied by heavenly creatures, and one says, "We do not know what things *look* like, as you say. We know what things *are* like. It must be a very limiting thing, this *seeing*." The most important part of that initial interview is getting past what people LOOK like. I'm not talking about physical appearance, although there are multiple studies on the effect of outward appearance and customer interaction. I'm talking about what they seem like. It is critical to forget what they LOOK like and get to what they ARE like very quickly. Usually, you spend a couple hours with someone before your company depends on them in some way. That's a big decision that we can learn to make from so many incredible bosses that have come before us.

You're only as good as the people you hire. —Ray Kroc, McDonald's

Satya Nadela, CEO of Microsoft, has two qualifications he seeks in candidates. He looks for clarity and energy. He says, "The people who are capable of getting into a situation where there is in some sense panic, and who can bring first clarity on what to do next—that is invaluable." Those people are able to cut through ambiguity and clearly define a problem and a solution. Those are people you want on your team. Clarity is only half of Nadela's equation. The other half is energy. A person who can cut through the noise, clearly identify and communicate the problem and get everyone on the same page of a solution is a whole person. Finding a candidate who is clear and brings energy to those around them is easy when you know what you're looking for. Keep a few interview questions that seek this out. Ask about work situations that felt difficult where no one knew what to do. Ask about their relationships with co-workers.

Warren Buffet is known for his unique management style. He looks for three key qualities: Integrity, energy and intelligence. He values integrity the most and says, "If you don't have the first, the other two will kill you. If you hire somebody without integrity, you really want them to be dumb and lazy." People with energy take initiative and motivate those around them. They raise the bar on productivity. People with intelligence have critical thinking and problem-solving abilities. Integrity is what keeps them honest and loyal. These are innate traits. People ARE intelligent. People ARE energetic. They have integrity. They can't be taught these things. Odds are, if these traits aren't found early on in the interview process, they won't be on display later. People can change, sure. But these aren't attributes you want to have to teach someone. This is the minimum standard.

Down through the years I have met people and immediately thought they were not relevant to my future, and I've met others who I thought would be game-changers but turned out to not be. Some people grow on you and others grow away from you. If I had been looking more closely at who they were, I would have made some different decisions and saved myself and my organization some trauma.

When I was first employed as a janitor at Calvary Church in Irving, Texas, there was a man there named Jack Pruitt who served as the Executive Pastor. He was flamboyant in his public speaking, was overly dramatic and his first impression was overwhelming. I wondered why my pastor had this guy on his staff. Yet five years later, as I moved from janitor to administrative assistant and then on to become the youth pastor of a megachurch, I learned the WHY. He was incredible with pastoral care. His love for people and loyalty to the church were far beyond excellence. His compassion and charity for people like me (at the bottom) were incredibly empowering and encouraging. I grew to love, respect and trust this man's friendship and heart. My first impression was wrong, but the process was right!

I have worked with others who initially I thought were all that, only to discover they were all talk and no results. I've had people who were fun to be around and hang out with but horrible to empower, because they continually failed to perform simple and clear tasks, and they always had an excuse. Those people not only didn't last long. They created waves that were unnecessary because they were disruptive from the very beginning.

On one occasion, I hired Mark. Mark was great in the interview process, but I quickly became frustrated with daily interactions. Every time I walked by his desk, he was just sitting there. It drove me crazy. Because his productivity didn't look like mine, I couldn't move past it to empowerment. I would come up with these jobs—some menial, some so difficult, I didn't think they could be done. No matter what I threw his way, he got it done. Well, he didn't do it himself. Mark had this ability to create teams of volunteers, to find people to get the job done. He wouldn't just get them to do the job. He would organize a system so that the job would get done by a team of people forever. He was a master delegator, but I lived in my frustration because I couldn't see what was happening past my own expectation of what it should look like. I didn't see his value at the time. Now, I wish I had 100 Marks.

If you don't know who you're hiring, then you can't know how to develop them. If you hire well, you can focus your energy on development and retention.

THE DEVELOPMENTAL PROCESS

The only thing worse than training your employees and having them leave is not training them and having them stay.
—Henry Ford, Ford Motor Company

Developing an employee is not just training them to perform their daily tasks. True development starts with evaluation and base lining. All employers should be giving their employees personality tests and assessments on an annual basis to determine who they are and their weaknesses. So many resources exist today, from DISC to Enneagrams to Myers-Briggs. The trend in the past has been to attend huge conferences. Time has shown that the most effective development happens on a small group level, and even better, at the individual level.

Assessment is one aspect, but having the ability to personally coach or hire a coach for employees results in immeasurable growth. Introspection is the absolute basis of personal growth. Managing introspection for your people allows them to remove their personal limitations. The largest hurdle I've seen is hesitation to change. All growth requires change in a positive direction. Removing fear from the equation generates this capacity for flexibility that is crucial to long-term, sustainable success. You'll never have a strong team unless you start with strong members.

Failure is the big F word in business. Good people don't want to fail. They don't want to make mistakes. It's not just a matter of hubris. Good people don't want to let their company or employer or co-workers down. It's important to let them fail. Failure should be an experience. All of us should encourage our employees to fail. Not all the time, of course, but teaching our people to fail correctly every once in a while is vital. If you give your employees the flexibility to fail the right way, you will set your team apart from your competition. Teach them to fail rarely, fail early, and fail when it doesn't matter. In other words, don't fail a lot. It should be rare and, hopefully, not intentional. Fail early. Don't wait until the last minute to fail. If you fail at the end of a project, there's no recovery—it's too late to come back. Teach them to fail when the stakes aren't too high. If you fail when everything is on the line, the damage is almost irreversible. But if you fail in the beginning, on the first idea, with an intentional audience, it doesn't feel like failure. It feels like a learning experience. It feels like growth.

Professional development and personal development make employees feel invested in your organization and your vision. Hiring is about capability and potential. Development is about execution and growth, but empowerment is about longevity.

THE EMPOWERING PROCESS

When people are financially invested, they want a return. When people are emotionally invested, they want to contribute. —Simon Sinek, author *Start with Why: How Great Leaders Inspire Everyone to Take Action*

Empowerment is the buzz word of the year. It's this overarching concept that we as people need to encourage others to do and be. Empowerment is more than that. It's encouragement, sure, but it truly is the releasing of your people to not only execute your vision, but to echo your vision. When you have the right people, developing and growing in the right way, you trust them to go out into the world or within your company to bring in more right people and develop others. The healthiest organizations are not micro-managed. In fact, the healthiest economies across the world are not under dictatorships. Prosperity and success lay in the hands of people. If you get hiring and development right, empowerment is just the grease that keeps the wheels turning.

Empowered employees aren't working for a paycheck or acclaim. They're working for themselves. Empowered employees don't work FOR you, they work WITH you. You can empower anyone, but the secret is doing it at the right time.

A 2018 study in the Harvard Business Journal demonstrated that empowering leaders didn't have an effect on their employees' abilities to perform daily tasks, but it did have an effect on their employees' work ethic, treatment of others, and overall morale or energy. Daily tasks are based on skills, and the rest is personal and requires the right attitude. That's where empowerment bridges the gap. Give them more responsibility. Let them feel helpful. Let them work on hard things. I said before, employees are kind of like children. Everyone likes to feel like they're big enough to contribute.

Empowerment can be done wrong. Empowering the wrong person at the wrong time can result in them feeling burdened by maybe an increased workload or a complicated situation. Empowering someone who doesn't quite understand the vision can result in frustrations and miscommunications. Empowering a disgruntled employee can result in division and drama. If you're hiring right and developing your people, you should be attuned enough to know when an employee is off or going through a difficult time and may need a different approach or a break.

I recently heard a manager tell a story of how he almost fired an employee who wasn't getting her work done. When he was discussing this with another manager, they realized no one had checked in with her in almost six months. After a one-on-one, he learned she had changed her personal goals and the work he was assigning her didn't align with them. He made a few adjustments to her workload, and her enthusiasm and productivity returned. Don't operate in management blind spots. Give your people access to you. It requires time, but the sacrifice is worth the reward.

As a pastor, I'm not called to just lead the people. I shepherd the people. Any leader should be the same way. You don't just give the orders. You have to care for your flock. A shepherd's primary responsibility is the safety and welfare of the flock. He manages their intake and output. He watches their moods for signs of sickness or lack of stimulation. He knows their relationships with other sheep, putting teams together and separating those who don't get along. Shepherds walk beside the sheep, through difficult and stressful situations, like shearing, that they know will benefit the sheep.

Once you get yourself mentally, physically, spiritually, emotionally, and intellectually healthy, you can get your people healthy. And once you get your people healthy, you can focus on the real strategic impact: the customer.

DESIGNING CUSTOMERS

Recently, I have noticed a significant drop in customer service. It seems as if over the past 3-5 years, the level of service I am experiencing is beyond comprehension. I have come to a personal resolution that I give any company and every company the "Maury Davis three-minute rule." It started with standing at a counter and not having one employee speak to me.

I stepped into a Mapco here in Nashville and noticed both employees stepping out of the store as I entered. I observed that one of them was getting in a car to leave and the other one was smoking a cigarette. I went through the store and grabbed a cup of coffee and a power bar. I then went and prepared to pay at the counter, only to find no employees were in the building—and even after eye contact through the exterior glass, no one came to take my money. I realized my time wasn't worth their interruption of a conversation and a smoke. I left the coffee and the power bar on the counter, only to be asked on the way out why I couldn't wait. I didn't say much, but I was shocked. Customers do not go to stores to wait on the employees. How do people think like that?

My next experience was in a McDonald's outside Atlanta where I stepped to the counter and waited. People were there doing things like getting coffee and bagging burgers, but no one even said, "Just a moment," or, "be right with you," or anything else. I waited three minutes and stepped across the street to another fast food restaurant. You may think that is being impatient or not tolerant, but I am the customer, and your service to me is a difference-maker.

This goes far beyond what people do. Maya Angelou said it best when she said, "I've learned that people will forget what you said, people will forget what you did, but people will never forget how you made them feel."

Stories of companies impacting customers' emotions is all over the news. The story of Kerry Drake and United Airlines came across my screen one night. He ran through the airport to make a connecting flight. It was important to him. He was going to spend the last moments with his dying mother. The flight attendants on his first plane had seen his distress. They notified the captain who made a call. When Drake was within 20 yards of his next flight, he heard, "Mr. Drake, we've been expecting you." The crew had delayed departure just for him. He was emotional. He made it in time. On the news story, the expert said, "Airline employees are evaluated based on their ability to keep a schedule. Airlines compete with each other on who has the best on-time departure record. When the crew on this flight heard about this distraught passenger trying to make his connection, they must have said, 'to hell with it'... and they made the right call."

Here is the bottom line: Walmart, Chick-fil-A, Kroger's, AutoZone, banks, car dealerships—even charities and churches—have to understand: we are in the PEOPLE business. Regardless of your field of employment, you're in the people business. Without a culture that makes people feel welcomed and valued, the "product" is minimized or irrelevant.

Part of a leader's assignment is helping those he leads understand how to welcome, serve, treat, and respect people. It needs to be the DNA of any organization. Little things matter!

"Catch the foxes for us, the little foxes that are spoiling the vineyards, while our vineyards are in blossom." — Song of Solomon 2:15

I meet people all the time who think little things in service, excellence, and presentation do not make a difference. I have studied enough, lived long enough and been educated enough by growth specialists to know that theory is wrong.

I served as a pastor for almost 28 years, and during that time, I determined that the little things affected the big picture more than most people know. So often, we become comfortable with the status quo, rather than viewing things from the customers' or congregants' views.

Upon arriving at Cornerstone Church in 1991, I found a small, struggling church on a gravel parking lot with a building that had seen better days. The current attendees were happy, passionate and had a great dream, but their understanding of increasing traffic was limited. I had the church board walk with me through the building, around the building and across the grounds and look at everything from a visitors' point of view. They looked with fresh eyes at painting, landscaping, layout and the physical appearance. Much like someone having guests at their house or preparing to sell a house, the little things become tasks to be cleaned up or fixed before sale. Get your house in order.

Let's look at the three areas that attract, maintain and elevate a customer's commitment to your brand.

LOCATION AND CURB APPEAL

Have you ever walked into a hotel lobby and said … WOW? Do you remember your first trip to Disney World, Universal Studio's, Sea World or Six Flags over Texas? The minute you walk through the doors or turnstiles, the world changes into a different environment, atmosphere and experience.

I live in Nashville, Tennessee—famous for the Opryland Hotel, the flagship Gaylord property. I have lived here for over 30 years, and whenever I go to an activity, a dinner, a banquet or even just meet someone for coffee, I love going in. The botanical garden atmosphere, the waterfalls and indoor river boat rides, the gardens, flower beds and trees that have been growing for decades is spectacular. The perpetual growth cycle for plants comes from a totally and carefully controlled atmosphere. The WOW factor comes from intentionality, attention to details and determination to be the best.

The founder of McDonald's was asked years ago what he thought McDonald's greatest value was and his response surprised people. It wasn't burgers or Ronald McDonald's image. It was location, location, location.

Recently, my wife and I went to eat at one of my favorite restaurants, and the first thing we noticed was the uncleanliness that we had never observed. It wasn't just the air that smelled bad. The floors were not clean and most of the tables and booths were partially wiped. The sad truth is, after years of being a loyal customer, that one experience began a process of not going back. The truth is we tried it again a few weeks later and decided there were too many clean restaurants that cared enough about their customers and their public reputation.

Location and curb appeal may not seem "spiritual" to the person of faith, but everyone who might visit your church isn't a person of faith. As a matter of fact, if people that are just "seeking" aren't coming to your church, WHY are you open? You can make the argument that people shouldn't be so shallow, so judgmental, so opinionated—but the truth is there are multiple personalities driving past your place of ministry or business and your ability to reach more people faster determines your growth, your fruitfulness, your influence and ultimately, in the business world, your income.

Mowing the yard matters. Making sure your advertisement and signage is current, informative and inspirational are all important. A clean exterior and interior all have an initial impact on your first-time consumer or potential congregant.

Your most unhappy customers are your greatest source of learning. —Bill Gates

You may wonder how you are doing in this area as a leader. I recommend you gather a group of people from within and without and create a survey to ask the tough questions about location, curb appeal and first impressions. A collective group of people will, in all likelihood, identify things that you as the primary leader won't. Odds are, they won't focus just on physicality. You'll begin to learn breakdowns in your process for bringing in new people. You'll learn about issues with your people who are working on the front lines. You'll find their strengths and weaknesses.

I remember after 20 years of leading a successful church, I became totally comfortable with our staging, structure and policies—only to discover that those that served well for a decade became a hurdle to a generation that had shifted the culture from boomers to millennials. The perpetual oversight of presentation is critical to continued relevance and growth.

FIRST IMPRESSIONS AND FEELINGS

Let me make sure we both understand exactly what I mean by those two terms. To me, first impressions are what people experience from a welcoming and helpful atmosphere that comes from people and their congeniality. From the time a person steps out of their vehicle or steps on the property, their experience begins. Hospitality is a big deal. How people are greeted and invited into the business or church affects their attitude. I wish that my attitude was always positive, upbeat and happy, but somedays it isn't. What is even worse is when an employee takes an attitude of hope and squashes it through rudeness or abrupt dismissal of helping you.

It takes months to find a customer ... seconds to lose one.
—Vince Lombardi

Recently, I went to purchase an outside gas grill for our new deck, and we entered into a well-known entity famous for garden equipment, building supplies, etc. The floor man greeted us and gave us a first-class tour through the grills, explaining the positives and negatives of each model. We finally decided on one, and he gave us the ticket to take to the counter and pay for it. He told us once we had our receipt, he would put one together in the back. We stepped up to pay and told the cashier that we were going to pay and get it put together. He never asked who told us that. He simply said we aren't assembling anything till the middle of the week. I said, "The man in the department said he would do it after we were receipted." He responded with exasperation and frustration. "I said, we aren't doing that on weekends ... period." I was a little amazed at the lack of customer awareness, the inability to explain or even rationally discuss the issue.

We walked away because our first impression was affected by the company Scrooge. Not only were we frustrated with the confusing messages, but the final straw of treating us like we were too stupid to understand what he said the first time affected our mood. *Mine in particular!* I could have asked myself what this man might be going through, what made him so rude and disrespectful and so dismissive of someone ready to spend hundreds of dollars...but I just walked away. One hour later, I purchased another grill from the business across the street and had a perfect experience.

Just think, in a national chain with an incredible reputation, one person on the front line can affect your traffic, your income and your growth. Parking lot attendants, ushers and greeters all make a first impression. The teacher at the school, the Walmart greeter, the gas station attendant, as well as every other first-line employee control the image and the reputation of your company or church. Customer service is not a department. Customer service is every person who interfaces with another person. Before a person ever hears your music, hears your sermon or meets the pastor, they have already developed an impression of who you are based on the volunteers they have had interaction with. Watch a visiting family take their children to the nursery or elementary age children's service and look at the impact they have at check-in. While you are checking children in, moms and dads are checking you out!

One of my consultants did an evaluation of our First Impressions ministry at Cornerstone years ago. I was so disappointed when he pointed out that many of our door greeters talked to each other more than greeted. Our ushers didn't open the door with their hands, but they butt-bumped the door while they were carrying on personal conversations with one another.

We all know we enjoy being made welcome, and we as a visitor for the first time always feel a little awkward anyway. So that first impression with greeting and assistance are critical to moving from butterflies to expecting great things.

A warm and hospitable welcome creates a feeling of honor and respect and begins a connection that this is a place I like. The truth is, it all happens prior to the first delivery of message or product. A person's ability to receive your message or your product is greatly and maybe permanently affected by their first impression and personal consideration for how you make them feel.

VALUE ADDED

Have you ever asked yourself the question as a leader, "What is the valuable I am delivering?" As a pastor, it should be salvation, grace, love, peace, joy faith and eternal life. The hope that nothing in the world has to offer. When people walk into the doors of a house of worship, they do not come in for a place to get out of the rain, but in almost every instance a place to find freedom from pain. They are dealing with difficult situations, broken relationships, financial crisis and medical diagnosis that need something more than a counselor, a CPA, attorney or medical professional. They need a supernatural experience, and they instinctively know the church was birthed on earth from heaven for that very reason. The older I have become, the more I realize people do not need more education in church. They need more transformation and powerful experiences with God and His people.

Every company has a "product" which customers either need or want.

All products need to have the following three attributes:

1. QUALITY

All products must be of quality. You can't build excellence with a partially completed product or idea. Time needs to be spent on developing your product or service. Beyond having a fully fleshed-out product, building a quality culture is fundamental in a world where competition is brimming. It's the basis for setting yourself apart. In order to build a culture of quality, look at your customers as part of the company. Everyone is on the ship together, from buildings to employees to vendors and suppliers to customers. Everyone should win. Quality relies on accessible information. There are no secrets in the pursuit to excellence. Communication must be frequent and honest. There are successes and failures, sure. But more accurately, there are experiences from which to learn what was done right and what was done wrong. What worked well and what fell apart?

2. A DELIVERY SYSTEM

Once you have a product or service worthy of your customers, the delivery system is next. How are you getting it to the end user and what is their perception of it? Focus groups, test runs, friends and family nights—these are all tools to assess your delivery system. Is your system efficient AND effective? You're not delivering a product. You're delivering a solution. The delivery system is where customer service is initially implemented. It's the first interface with the end user, but it's not the last.

3. CUSTOMER LOYALTY

Customer loyalty stems from the follow-through and the follow-up! One of my favorite stories of customer loyalty happened in my own hometown. A woman by the name of Christina McMenemy stayed every year in Opryland Hotel for a conference. And every year, she loved the clock radio that played spa sounds. She searched high and low for it and even messaged the company, only to find out that the clock radio wasn't sold in stores. When she checked in for her annual conference the next year, there were two clocks—one, a gift to her. Over the moon, she said "You re-affirmed that there are still companies out there focused on great service, and you've made a lifelong fan out of me." I can assure you that Christina cared more about being seen and valued than she did about actually getting a clock. Customer loyalty isn't difficult to attain if you're intentional in your products quality and customer service mentality. Anyone in business knows it's more cost effective and beneficial in the long run to retain a customer than seek a new one. Retained customers are free marketing and get the new customer for you. Your employees work for you. Let the customer work for you, too. The camaraderie alone makes the enterprise feel bigger than it may be.

Growth requires that you're investing in yourself as a leader. It mandates that you invest in your employees. It's only possible if you're investing in your customers. The secret to all of the success, the magic ingredient is consistency. Once you have the perfect team, growth strategies, and a solid product or service, the only way to grow as a leader and business is through consistently delivering an excellent product with excellent customer service. Consistency allows you to measure effectiveness. Consistency establishes your reputation. Most importantly, consistency maintains your message. It's not rocket science. It's commitment.

PART FOUR: STRATEGIC MARKETING

by Martijn van Tilborgh

4.1

IDENTIFY

EVERYTHING STARTS WITH identifying your message. What is the unique value proposition God has given you? What value does your calling bring to those around you? Knowing who you are in Christ is the most important, and most difficult part of this process. We start with identity and purpose.

This may sound simple, but many I have worked with struggle to answer these questions. Top-level influencers struggle to identify what they have to offer. Sure, most of them know how to give a generic answer; but this question needs to be answered with precision. What sets you apart from everyone else?

JESUS KNEW HIS IDENTITY

Jesus knew who He was. He knew the specific value He brought to His target audience. We read about it in Luke 4:16-19:

So He came to Nazareth, where He had been

*brought up. And as His custom was, He went into
the synagogue on the Sabbath day, and stood up to
read. And He was handed the book of the prophet
Isaiah. And when He had opened the book, He found
the place where it was written:*
"The Spirit of the Lord is upon Me,
Because He has anointed Me
To preach the gospel to the poor;
He has sent Me to heal the brokenhearted,
To proclaim liberty to the captives
And recovery of sight to the blind,
To set at liberty those who are oppressed;
To proclaim the acceptable year of the Lord."

Isn't that amazing? Jesus didn't come with a generic, one-size-fits-all message. He knew who He was, and spoke with confidence about what he had to offer to specific people. His message was not abstract. It was practical and clear, tailored toward his target audience.

This is what we can learn from Jesus' ministry:

- Jesus knew He was anointed and called by God with a specific gift. He was able to confidently proclaim who He was.

- He understood His message, and its specific value proposition, as He brought good news, healing, liberty and sight.

- He knew His target audience: the ones who would most benefit from the value He was offering. He knew they were the poor, the brokenhearted, the captives, the blind, and the oppressed.

Jesus' message was clear. One of His target audiences was the blind. What was His value proposition? You don't have to be blind anymore! Another target demographic was the poor. What was His value proposition to them? You don't have to be poor anymore! Jesus was specific in who He was, who He was trying to reach, and how He was going to help them solve their problems.

What is your unique message and gift? What is the value you have to offer? Who are the people who will most benefit from your message? To whom are you sent?

Jesus knew how to answer those questions. Do you?

THE MANIFOLD WISDOM OF GOD

It's all about knowing who you are, and articulating it in a way helps the people you're called to reach. God chose to give each and every person a measure of that His value to steward. God's distribution strategy is to use us, His body.

The Bible teaches us the following in Ephesians 3:8-11:

To me, who am less than the least of all the saints, this grace was given, that I should preach among the Gentiles the un-searchable riches of Christ, and to make all see what is the fellowship of the mystery, which from the beginning of the ages has been hidden in God who created all things through Jesus Christ; to the intent that now the manifold wisdom of God might be made known by the church to the principalities and powers in the heavenly places, according to the eternal purpose which He accomplished in Christ Jesus our Lord.

This portion of scripture doesn't talk about a "singular" wisdom; it speaks of "manifold" wisdom. There are so many sides to God's creative expression that it's impossible for one human to display them. In fact, collectively as humanity, we still aren't able to define the boundaries of His creative expression: He does more than what we can even think or imagine.

In our limited mindsets, we tend to create ministry templates that allow God to work through us in a limited set of rules we create for Him. Those parameters that we've defined make up only a sliver of the potential spectrum of possibility within God's reality.

Yet when we look at our churches, ministries, projects, and events, they all seem to look the same. Why is this? I like to think God is more creative than what we see happen in churches today. It's because we tend to fall into a deception that keeps us from seeing the full reality of the manifold wisdom of God. We fail to see our unique value proposition. We model after each other instead of trying to figure out who God says we are individually. The devil will make you believe uniformity is a virtue, but it isn't. It may have the appearance of godliness, but it has denied the power thereof.

I discovered this truth several years ago when I was teaching at a Bible college in Aruba, a small island in the Caribbean about forty miles from the coast of Venezuela. I taught for five days. At some point during that week, the church on the island organized a March for Jesus through the main streets of the island. Aruba is small, and has only about 110,000 people, with one major town where most of them live. The island is seven miles, wide and only about three to four miles deep. The churches had decided it would be a great statement of unity to march around the city, holding banners and singing songs about Jesus.

I remember standing by the side of the road as hundreds of people marched through the streets. They all wore red T-shirts, sang the same songs, marched on the same beat, and carried the same smiles on their faces. I guess their goal was to show the love of Jesus through these efforts, in hopes that others would be attracted to this display of "happiness and joy."

Now, I have no doubt that these people marched with a pure heart and an upright motivation. I honestly believe that. Yet, something was terribly off as I watched the crowds walk. It seemed so forced. Fake. It felt like it lacked authenticity. Their behavior of walking, singing, and smiling a certain way appeared to have the opposite effect of what they were trying to accomplish.

The random bystander on the street was not attracted by their behavior. In fact, they looked uncomfortable and often looked away in hopes that nobody would hand them one of those balloons or tracts they were carrying. Suddenly, it hit me. God is not looking for uniformity! He's looking for diversity. His value for mankind is manifested through the unique value He puts in each of us. He is looking for a unique expression of His manifold wisdom through every individual. Instead of trying to have us all do the same thing, He wants us all to start doing something different!

This was a real eye-opener for me. For so long, I was taught that true unity was created through uniformity. In that moment, I started to see the difference between the two. I realized that the opposite is true. True unity is not accomplished through uniformity; it is accomplished through diversity. Diversity will only manifest fully if each of us find our lane.

So let me ask you again...

- What is your gift?
- What is your message?
- What is your unique value proposition?
- What is your lane?
- Who are you called to be?
- Who are you called to?

Joel 2:7-11 says this:

They run like mighty men,
They climb the wall like men of war;
Every one marches in formation,
And they do not break ranks.
They do not push one another;
Every one marches in his own column.
Though they lunge between the weapons,
They are not cut down.
They run to and fro in the city,
They run on the wall;
They climb into the houses,
They enter at the windows like a thief.
The earth quakes before them,
The heavens tremble;
The sun and moon grow dark,
And the stars diminish their brightness.
The Lord gives voice before His army,
For His camp is very great;

For strong is the One who executes His word.

This scripture describes the army of the Lord the way it is intended to be. No person in this army breaks rank. Nobody pushes one another. Everyone is in their own lane, doing their own unique thing, without competing. And in doing so, they are one. Unity is the result of each individual finding their own place within the army. No rank is the same. No position is equal. It's uniquely designed for each individual to march. And as we march in that unique, authentic way, we become one.

This phase is all about giving birth to the very thing for which God created you.

We don't tend to promote this in our ministries and churches. More often than not, we operate in wineskins, structures, and leadership models that don't facilitate the kind of environment where identification can take place.

THE THREE LEVELS OF REVELATION

There is an interesting story in the Bible, in which Peter converses with Jesus one day. We find it in Matthew chapter 18. Let's read it:

When Jesus came into the region of Caesarea Philippi, He asked His disciples, saying, "Who do men say that I, the Son of Man, am?" So they said, "Some say John the Baptist, some Elijah, and others Jeremiah or one of the prophets." He said to them, "But who do you say that I am?" Simon Peter answered and said, "You are the Christ, the Son of the living God." Jesus answered and said to him, "Blessed are you, Simon Bar-Jonah, for flesh and blood has not revealed this to you, but My Father who is in heaven. And I also say to you that you are Peter, and on this rock I will build My church, and the gates of Hades shall not prevail against it. (Matthew 18:13-18)

I'd heard this story many times, and thought it was a cool story. However, after hearing it one too many times, I started to get bored. How many times can you listen to the same sermon without getting bored?

My boredom was short-lived after I got a revelation from this portion of scripture which I had never recognized. It forever revolutionized the way I look at things. Let's paraphrase the story a bit as we unpack it. Jesus is sitting down with Peter one day. They are having a conversation. Jesus asks him:

"Hey Peter, tell me, what is the word on the street?"

Peter answers, "What do you mean, Lord?"

Jesus: "Well, who do the people say I am? Tell me, what stories are being told about who I am. What's the word on the street?"

Peter: "Well, actually, there are quite a few stories going around about you, Lord. Some say that you're John the Baptist who came back from the dead. Others say you're Elijah or one of the prophets. I can't really answer that question since there are many, many stories going around from different people expressing different opinions!"

Jesus' question and Peter's answer is what I call a first-level understanding (or revelation), which we all have at some point in our walk with Christ. There's nothing wrong with it. In fact, there is a time in your faith walk when you simply believe what others say about Jesus. When you become a believer, you simply believe what the pastor tells you about Jesus is. There's nothing wrong with that—it's where we all start. But it becomes a problem when we stagnate and stay at that level. There is a higher level of revelation we all need to get to at some point in our walk with the Lord. Let's look at this Level Two revelation next.

Jesus: "Well, Peter, now that you know what other people say, let me ask you another question: Who do you say that I am?"

Wow. The questioning became personal. It no longer matters what others told Peter. It was now up to him to tap into a higher level of understanding, to answer that question for himself.

Peter answers: "You, sir, are the Christ! You are the Son of the living God!"

Jesus: "Oh, wow, Peter! I'm impressed. This is some information that you didn't get off the street. This is not something anyone has told you. This is pure revelation from the Father. He Himself must have revealed this to you, because this isn't public information."

Now, remember, when Peter answered this question, it wasn't public knowledge that Jesus was the Son of God. Nobody really knew who Jesus was at that time. The information Peter shared was the result of a supernatural experience with the Father. Peter had been given a revelation from God Himself, showing that Jesus was the Christ, the son of the living God! He didn't read it in the Bible like we do, because there was no Bible as we have it today! Pretty amazing, isn't it? Peter heard from God about who Jesus truly was! This was another level of revelation, far beyond what was heard in the streets. It was supernatural. It was personal. It was a game-changer for Peter.

When Christ is revealed to us on a personal level, that revelation becomes realer than any circumstance and reality around us. When this happens, you can truly start your walk with God.

And that's exactly what it is. You start your walk with God. This level cannot be our end goal. It's merely the starting point that puts you on a path to a third level of revelation...a level that no one ever seems to discuss.

You see, most church culture is crafted in order to get people to the second level of revelation. As leaders, we tend to make it our goal to help each person get a supernatural revelation of Jesus. We have come to believe that, once people get to this level, they have arrived. Guess what? It's not true. It's not true at all! It's really only the beginning.

I honestly believe that by making this second-level revelation our primary goal, we distract the church from being truly victorious. Why? Because on this level, we all are equal. Though necessary, this second level of revelation becomes the breeding ground for uniformity if we stay there too long.

The conversation Jesus had with Peter shifted the focus from Jesus to Peter. The first two levels of revelation were about Jesus; however, there was a third level Jesus wanted Peter to grasp that had nothing to do with Jesus. It had everything to do with Peter.

When Peter was ready to receive it, Jesus turned to him and said: "Peter, now that you know what other people are saying about Me, and now that you know, by revelation, who I am, it is time for you to understand something else. Let me tell you who you are! You are Peter, and on this rock I will build My church, and the gates of Hades shall not prevail against it."

Wow. Let's think about this for just a moment. For the first time in his life, Peter had a revelation about who he was supposed to be, as Jesus Himself identified him by uttering words of destiny and purpose over his life. Jesus declared the very thing that made Peter unique. He called him Peter (Rock), and with those words, He released a revelation of prophetic destiny over Peter.

It's this third-level revelation that we all need to have. It's this level of understanding that will truly make us all diverse—unique. We have to hear the same words Peter heard that day. The only difference in this third level of revelation is that the words are unique to each of us.

We need to come to a place where Jesus turns to us and says, "Now that you know what others say, and now that you know who I am, let me tell you who you are!" This supernatural revelation will propel us into our unique prophetic destiny. In fact, it's this level of understanding that becomes the foundation of the church, against which the gates of Hades can't prevail.

If we want to truly overthrow the gates of hell, we need to attain this level of revelation. This is where the action happens. On this level, the battle is won. This is the place where everyone in God's army finds his or her lane, position, and rank. It's power in diversity.

Know who you are. Identify the message God has given you. Be confident, demonstrating your unique value through the concise articulation of your message. Know your target audience, and what it is you offer that will help them with specific problems.

Once you answer these questions, you'll be ready for step two. In the next chapter, I'll help you make your message available to your target audience.

4.2

ATTENTION SHIFT

NOT TOO LONG ago I sat down with a pastor of a mega-church on the West coast. He had flown me out to pick my brain about some marketing related projects for his church and ministry. We were having dinner at a small restaurant in the downtown of the quaint California town where he had been a pastor for some time now.

We had a great time getting to know each other while enjoying some incredible food. Halfway through our conversation he made a statement followed by a question that I have become very familiar with while working with many great leaders over the years: "Even the most committed families in my church only show up 1.8 times every month."

"Wow, that must really be frustrating for you when you preach your 6-week sermon series," I remember responding. "How are people going to be fully benefiting from your series if they only hear the first and the fourth while missing out on the rest?"

I knew that making him feel the pain of his reality would cause him to think a little deeper about the real issue and its possible solution. The truth is, most (if not all) churches these days are dealing with the same dynamic. Ministries all over the country are struggling to get people back in the pews week after week. It's a trend that ministries big and small experience.

My pastor friend then asked me the following question: "How can you help me to get my people to show up every single week?" I quickly told him that I could not help him solve his problem. Sure, there are tons of gimmicky and manipulative marketing tricks that can be deployed to shame and guilt people back in their seats every Sunday. But is this really what we want to do?

The tragedy is not so much that this is an overall trend among churches, but more so that we don't seem to understand what's behind this trend: a great attention shift.

This is not something new. Attention shifts happen all the time. Not just in church, but in every industry and market, we experience waves of change as the attention of the people we're trying to reach shifts.

Shifts in attention make previous distribution models obsolete. We used to buy toys in stores, now we buy them online. We used to go to restaurants for the convenience of not having to cook. Now, we're ordering food on an app from restaurants that specialize in delivery only. We used to shop at K-Mart, call a taxi for transport and go to Blockbuster to rent a movie.

But guess what? The attention has shifted!

The church is not exempt from attention shifts. And the stats shared by my pastor friend are proving it. Instead of blaming our congregations for not showing up, we should ask ourselves what value we are offering to the people we're trying to reach. Are we giving people a reason to come back every week?

It's all about supply and demand. We're living in a free market enterprise. You see, the market is always right. According to our target audience, the value we're offering is only worth 1.8 Sundays of their precious time.

Yet we continue to build systems and structures around the assumption that the model we used for the last 50 years is the model we're going to have until Jesus comes back. We continue to invest our time, energy and money based on the assumption that our distribution model will remain the same.

Don't be fooled. We need to understand the shifts in attention we're going through as a society and as the church.

We need to have the courage to challenge the very thing that has been such a blessing to us for so many years. Just because something worked yesterday doesn't mean it's going to continue to work the same way. In fact, it never will. The world around us is always progressing. It's always advancing. And we had better make sure we advance with it.

In marketing we're always ask three questions:

- What is the value that I bring as an organization?

- Who can benefit most from that value?

- Where do I have the attention of those people?

As long as I can simply distribute value in the places and on platforms where I have the attention of the people who I am trying to reach, keeping them engaged with me as a ministry or organization will be easy.

IT'S SIMPLE, BUT IT'S NOT EASY!

We all like the idea of change, yet few of us like the manifestation of change. Yes, change is the only constant we can expect as we move into the future.

As leaders we need to,

Recognize change: We need to be able to discern and recognize when the attention of our people is shifting. Statistics like the one discussed here should be an indicator that we need to shift as the attention shifts.

Embrace change: We can't just watch the world change around us and merely be a bystander who observes others go through it. We need to fully embrace the new thing that is unfolding right in front of us.

Anticipate change: Just because things changed once, doesn't mean they won't change again. God will lead us into change all the time to keep moving us forward. We need to get to a point at which we start to anticipate change and expect it to come to us.

Become a change agent: The Bible teaches us that we're the head and not the tail. As Christian leaders we need to be those who lead the pack—those who lead the frontlines of innovation and progress.

Attention is shifting. Change is happening. And as church and marketplace leaders we're not exempt from its repercussion.

Let me give you a biblical illustration to shed some spiritual light on the matter, as well as some practical suggestions on how to navigate shifts in attention. There is an interesting passage in the book of Judges that talks about the rise of Deborah, the woman who became the leader of Israel in a time when the attention of the people was shifting. Deborah was the one who ended up guiding God's people through a major attention shift.

Let's read about it in Judges 5: 6-8 (NKJV):

"In the days of Shamgar, son of Anath,
In the days of Jael,
The highways were deserted,
And the travelers walked along the byways.
Village life ceased, it ceased in Israel,
Until I, Deborah, arose,
Arose a mother in Israel.
They chose new gods;
Then there was war in the gates.

Before we break down this scripture let's find out who Shamgar was. Shamgar isn't a popular biblical figure we learn about in kids' church. This doesn't mean he wasn't a good guy. In fact, the Bible gives us the following account of Shamgar in Judges 3:31:

After him was Shamgar the son of Anath, who killed six hundred men of the Philistines with an ox goad; and he also delivered Israel.

A DECENT DAY FOR GOD'S PEOPLE

As you can see, Shamgar was a pretty good fellow. He killed 600 Philistines with an ox goad. Quite impressive, I would say. He was also the one who delivered God's people.

All of that to say that under Shamgar's leadership, God's people experienced a season of prosperity—not much to complain about. Enemies were being killed. Israel was living in freedom.

Things were alright.

Yet, even though things were decent during the days of Shamgar, things began to shift. The days of Shamgar's success created a false sense of security that everything would be like this forever. An illusion that nothing would ever change.

Yet, in the days of Shamgar three things happened:

THE HIGHWAYS WERE DESERTED

Highways are places of attention. It's the most popular way to travel from point A to point B. Highways represent "efficiency." They are the fastest way to get somewhere. Highways are created for attention, and when attention shifts, highways get deserted.

What once was the place to be, no longer serves the same purpose it once did. It just sits there being empty cause the people who once showed up are no longer putting the same value on its function. They are no longer willing to trade their time for its benefit.

I used to think that if you always do what you always did, you will always get what you always got. That the same action would give us the same result indefinitely. The truth is much more complicated than that. As a matter of fact, if you always do what you always did, you will get less and less from the same efforts. As the world and culture around us is changing our efforts become less and less effective until the places that once were highways become deserted altogether.

TRAVELERS WALKED ALONG THE BYWAYS

We need to meet people where they are at. When the highways we once had are no longer serving the community we're trying to reach, they often end up in places that are not made to get them to their destination fast. As leaders we are called to develop new highways to accommodate the people we are called to and give them a way to get to their destination in the least amount of time.

As leaders we need create new opportunities for our target audience to connect with the value we have to offer as a ministry. We need to innovate and turn byways into highways as we add value to those we're called to serve. We need to be willing to leave the old behind us, even if "the old" gave us the success that got us to where we are today.

VILLAGE LIFE CEASED

Village life talks about community. When we are unwilling to shift with the changes that are happening around us, village life will cease to exist.

Village life is the community of people you do life with. When the people you try to serve in your ministry don't experience a sense of community it will be the beginning of the end. How do you facilitate an environment that is conducive to village life in an ever changing world?

Fifty years ago, village life was defined by those living within the same geographical proximity. In other words, your village consisted out of those you lived close to. Your neighbors, the people down the street, the baker on the corner. In other words, your village was defined by those you lived close to.

Then village life shifted in the 70s and 80s where you didn't necessarily have a sense of community with those who lived in your street, but more with those you worked with, you went to school with, you played tennis with etc. These people didn't necessarily live close to you, but they did life with you in other places.

Today, my 14-year-old son has friends he never sees in person. He relates to those he will never meet in a digital environment online. Does that make it less real? No, it doesn't. It's just different. Village life ceases to exist if we're unable to navigate the attention shift.

BE LIKE DEBORAH

Deborah was able to navigate the attention shift. She rose up as a mother in Israel and as implied by the context of this scripture brought an end to the three negatives above. We need to be like Deborah and shift our efforts from doing what we've always done to figuring out where our people are at today. Meet them in their needs and offer value where they are at.

Let's create new highways and reinstate true village life by embracing change and anticipating the changes of the future.

EXPECT WAR IN THE GATES

Verse 8 of Judges 6 talks about "war in the gates." Even Deborah experienced conflict. Expect resistance when you embrace change. It's part of the process. But when you do, it will be worth it at the end. Innovation will challenge status quo thinking, but will ultimate result into new paradigms and ways to better serve those we are called to.

4.3

THE LAST THING YOU NEED

THIS IS THE conclusion I came to after building 200 websites for my clients. I can't believe it took that long to come to this conclusion; once I did, it seemed so obvious.

After my $60K in debt, come-to-Jesus moment, I knew something had to change. Our current household income at the time, coupled with our attempts to save, wasn't enough. I knew I had to make more money somehow.

At the peak of my desperation, the Lord led me to 2 Kings 4:1-7, where we read about the prophet Elisha and a widow:

The wife of a man from the company of the prophets cried out to Elisha, "Your servant my husband is dead, and you know that he revered the Lord. But now his creditor is coming to take my two boys as his slaves."

Elisha replied to her, "How can I help you? Tell me, what do you have in your house?"

"Your servant has nothing there at all," she said, "except a small jar of olive oil."

Elisha said, "Go around and ask all your neighbors for empty jars. Don't ask for just a few. Then go inside and shut the door behind you and your sons.

Pour oil into all the jars, and as each is filled, put it to one side."

She left him and shut the door behind her and her sons. They brought the jars to her and she kept pouring. When all the jars were full, she said to her son, "Bring me another one."

But he replied, "There is not a jar left." Then the oil stopped flowing.

She went and told the man of God, and he said, "Go, sell the oil and pay your debts. You and your sons can live on what is left."

The widow in the story is in a hopeless situation. Her circumstances have led her onto a path where she accumulates a tremendous amount of debt. The situation is totally hopeless. There simply isn't a way out for her unless God intervenes. And He does!

The prophet asked her a simple question: "Tell me, what do you have in your house?"

This question is profound. It implies that, even in the most desperate situation, there is something "in your house" with which God can move. When Elisha asks the question, the widow is forced to think about the answer. She's pushed to identify the very thing that would become the vehicle of her deliverance.

A small jar of olive oil: something seemingly insignificant became a weapon of war that would lead her to victory, favor, and incredible abundance. It would not only bless her, but also leave a legacy for the next generation.

WHAT'S YOUR OIL?

When I read this story, I heard the Lord ask about my house. What did I have in my house that He could use to multiply? I thought about it long and hard. I'd never had an education. My Dutch army experience wasn't much help on this side of the pond. Really, I didn't see a lot to work with in my house.

Then, I remembered that, several years back, I'd picked up a book at Books-A-Million. I literally read it cover to cover. It was a book on Adobe Photoshop 6. I picked it up from the sales table, because Adobe 7 had come out at the time (for those who don't know what Photoshop is, it's the leading photo editing software on the market). Ninety-percent of the features in Photoshop 7 were the same as Photoshop 6, so it pretty much taught me the basics of graphic design. I'd used this new skill over the previous few years to do some basic graphics for the ministry in which I was involved. They definitely hadn't been award-winning designs, but I knew enough to be dangerous.

Something else came to mind. Several years back, I'd taken a job at a company called New Horizons Computer Learning Centers. With over 300 locations worldwide, New Horizons was the largest IT training company in the world. I had joined the sales team in the city of Utrecht, Netherlands, where they had just opened a new office. I had no experience whatsoever in B2B sales, but for some reason, they thought I was the man for the job. Boy, did I learn a lot. I discovered I was good at this sales thing. Within four months, I had broken two wall of fame sales records. My boss was ecstatic.

As I thought about these two opportunities, something in me came alive. My mind was spinning. Could it be that this was my "oil"? Photoshop expertise coupled with a sales background?

The excitement took over and turned into what I can only call a supernatural confidence. This could actually work! With my sales and graphic design background, I could probably figure out how to build a website. I had no clue how to do it; but if I put my mind to it, surely I could figure it out. I picked up the classified ads and started calling local businesses who appeared to have no online presence. It didn't take long before I'd made my first sale.

One of my first projects was to build a website for a local storage company called Lake Mary Mini Storage. I sold this project for $299. This wasn't going to get me out of my situation, but it was definitely a start. Before long, I had gotten pretty good at web development. Acquiring new business somehow came easily to me. There was never a lack of projects. I had this huge goal that, maybe, someday, I could make $4,000/month building these websites. Deep inside of me, I believed God would multiply my oil.

Four months later I reached my goal. Four months after that, I doubled that goal. A year later, I doubled it again—and again, a year after that. Eventually, I was generating millions of dollars doing business in the digital space.

BILLBOARDS IN THE DESERT

Something interesting happened. As I started to look at the Google analytics of my clients, I discovered that 60-80% of all web traffic to any given website would "bounce." This basically means most people decide to leave a website within 5 seconds of arriving.

This was extremely disturbing to me. By far, the majority of all traffic didn't stay long enough for my clients to tell their stories. Five seconds was not enough for anyone to engage an audience.

In other words, 99% of the websites we built didn't contribute measurably to the company's bottom line results. The thought was depressing. As a company, we were taking in good money from clients who never recouped their investment.

We were in the business of creating "billboards in the desert."

These sites looked all pretty and cool, but nobody cared. Nobody bothered to truly look at them. It didn't take me long to reach the conclusion that websites, in most cases, are a money pit that only takes from businesses—they don't give back.

The question I couldn't get out of my mind was this: "What can I do to retain people long enough that I can tell my story?" In other words, how do I draw people in? What visual and non-visual language do I use? What is the trick? I became obsessed with finding these answers.

HOW TO KEEP PEOPLE ENGAGED FOR MORE THAN 5 SECONDS

People ask three questions when they stumble upon a web page. All three demand an answer. If we fail to answer these questions effectively within five seconds, our audience will bounce.

Now, our audience is probably not aware that they are asking these questions, but on a subconscious level, they are.

The world of the web is fast. How many times do you search something on Google, click a link, and decide in mere seconds that this is not what you're looking for? People are in a rush. They're looking for information and they want it now. There is little patience. If we know what questions to answer, we'll have a significant advantage.

Here are the three questions:

1) WHERE AM I?

This may be obvious to you, but it's not obvious to someone who has never heard about you. You have one chance to make a first impression. There are a multitude of reasons people end up on your page. Whatever the reasons, we have to assume they don't know much about you. We have to master the skill of defining our organization in one sentence. Remember the term "elevator pitch"? This is like that, only shorter. Within seconds, someone has to be able to understand who it is they're dealing with. You can't tell your life story. No time for it. Don't even try. All you need to do is give them enough to satisfy the question, and do so in an engaging way.

2) WHAT CAN I DO HERE?

Really, the question is, what do you want them to do? You create your call to action based on your objective. Don't clutter your page with too many calls to action. Prioritize. Determine what's most important. If you only have one shot, what do you want to ask them? When you ask, show them the value behind that ask. Give them a reason to say yes.

3) WHY SHOULD I DO THIS WITH YOU?

Third-party credibility is important. Anything that adds credibility from the outside builds a foundation of trust and rapport. Build affiliations with organizations who have more name recognition. Get testimonials from those you've helped. Serve in a way to garner five-star reviews of your products and services.

When I started to implement strategy based on my newfound understanding, I saw bounce rates drop. It was a good start, but it wasn't the solution to the bigger issue I was trying to solve. How did I create measurable, bottom-line results? It required being known as the guy who helps people generate money (not the guy who takes their money).

Even though I was able to retain traffic significantly longer on a web page, this still wasn't enough for people to develop enough trust and desire. The simple truth is that people are not looking for an opportunity to spend money with anyone. It's going to take more than a visit on a website. There has to be that foundation of trust before people are willing to grab their wallet and swipe that card.

AUDIENCE DEVELOPMENT AND DATA BUILDING

Back in the early days of the internet, websites were developed to broadcast information. If I wanted information, I simply visited a website in hopes of finding it. It was based on one-way communication. The website would talk to the visitor. The visitor wouldn't talk back. In today's world, the internet is all about relationship— connection. Websites only play a small part, as the internet is much larger than websites (more on this later).

I discovered that, if I wanted to further my conversation after people leave my web page, I needed to establish some sort of connection that would allow me to do so. The moment someone hit my page should be the beginning of a relationship that continues after they leave. My main objective was to put myself in the driver's seat: to be in a position where I could further the conversation on my terms. I no longer wanted to be dependent on people coming to me. I wanted to go to them whenever I desired. The only way that would be possible was if I extracted information from visitors that allowed me to talk to them after they had left.

In today's world, information-gathering is accomplished in many different ways. There are multitudes of platforms that allow me to build an audience. I can talk to that audience whenever I want, without being dependent on them. It puts me in charge.

Email marketing remains one of the most effective communications. At the time I discovered these principles, I was focused mostly on email database building and marketing.

I decided to forget about websites altogether, and focus on landing pages with data assimilation. I built singular web pages with one objective: which was to build my audience database. We developed incredible strategies to optimize our conversion rates on these pages. We saw conversation rates of up to 82%, meaning that, out of every 100 people visiting our page, 82 would end up in our database. Pretty incredible.

LIFE CYCLE MARKETING

I started working with prominent organizations around the country to help them strategize and develop audiences in the same way. We helped many of them triple—or quadruple—their databases in a short time. Database building became our game.

It didn't take long for me to realize that, if you don't know how to further the conversation with new audiences, it doesn't really matter how much data you accumulate. Some of the biggest success stories we had still didn't have the desired bottom-line results. We were unable to engage our newfound audience.

In one such case, I helped a client build a database from scratch to over 100K in just a few months. We didn't use any advertising dollars; it was accomplished simply by leveraging existing influence. However, when it came time to sell to this audience, the results were far below where they should have been. I realized, painfully, that "the perfect customer" never walks in the door as the perfect customer. They are developed over time. Nobody comes into your database ready to buy.

For example: Let's look at your perfect customer. Let's call him Johnny.

Johnny has been a client for years. He didn't just buy from you once. He bought from you over and over again. Not only that, but Johnny also increased the frequency with which he bought, as well as his level of financial engagement. To top it off, he's is telling all his friends about his experience as he buys from you, and talking about it on social media.

We wish everybody could be like Johnny. Right? They can be!

The truth is that Johnny was developed over time. If we identify Johnny's customer journey and pinpoint what made him into Johnny, we can reverse-engineer the process. We can expose other leads to those same circumstances.

What turned Johnny from a cold lead into a raving fan? There were stepping stones along the way. It's important to map out your sales cycle, and identify the stepping stones one needs to take in order for a lead to move deeper into the cycle. Everything has a cycle. You can't shortcut the process; it requires patience.

If I know what turned Johnny into Johnny, I can engineer a process that will create more Johnnys. I just need to make sure that my calls to action are reasonable enough for my prospects to answer them. For example, I can't ask someone who just came in cold turkey to refer his friends to me. That doesn't make sense. We have no history yet. This is all common sense, but we all tend to be impatient.

There is a natural process, made up of seven phases, that defines each sales cycle. This process is uniform for any product and any industry. However, you need to be able to apply it to your product, service or organization.

Life cycle marketing is where I landed with my business. I embraced web development, but this time, in the context of the bigger picture. I help experts and leaders develop not only a website, but a comprehensive marketing blueprint tailored to their organization's objective.

Life Cycle Marketing is all about creating a world that will allow you to build an audience, and turn that audience into Johnnys. Believe me, it can be done! I've done it over and over again.

In the next chapter, I'll break down the typical customer life cycle into the seven phases, and help you apply these phases to your brand and product.

CONCLUSION

Whether you started on page one or fifty, whether you read two chapters or 12—we hope that the information presented here EXPANDED your world. You have chosen to expose your mind to the thinking of four people who all have the same goal through this project—to help you succeed!

The systems and structures that you develop in your organization serve to propel the mission you have set out. It is important to be aware of the current stage in the life cycle of your organization and adapt so that you can grow, and grow faster! These systems and structures function best inside the context of a healthy organization. The key factors that contribute to this health include culture, safety, trust, clarity, and collaboration. Leaders who ensure that these areas are addressed see productivity increases. Once these areas are functioning at healthy levels, we can focus on growth. Growth also follows a pattern in the organization: first, you must focus on growing yourself! Then, you can develop employees to function at optimal levels as well as focus on customer growth. One of the paths to growth includes marketing strategies. First, identify the message you want to share—who are you? Next, realize where the market is. Shifts in attention have led to the need for fast changing strategies and engineering to hold onto a person long enough to share your message.

No matter which area you find yourself needing more expansion, we hope that the information contained in this resource will be helpful to you. At any point in your process of growth in these areas, we are available to assist with detailed expertise.